The

Reference

Shelf

The American Prison System

Edited by Peter G. Herman

The Reference Shelf
Volume 73 • Number 5

The H.W. Wilson Company
2001

The Reference Shelf

The books in this series contain reprints of articles, excerpts from books, addresses on current issues, and studies of social trends in the United States and other countries. There are six separately bound numbers in each volume, all of which are usually published in the same calendar year. Numbers one through five are each devoted to a single subject, providing background information and discussion from various points of view and concluding with a subject index and comprehensive bibliography that lists books, pamphlets, and abstracts of additional articles on the subject. The final number of each volume is a collection of recent speeches, and it contains a cumulative speaker index. Books in the series may be purchased individually or on subscription.

Library of Congress has cataloged this serial title as follows:

The American prison system / edited by Peter G. Herman.
    p. cm—(The reference shelf ; v. 73, no. 5)
  Includes bibliographical references and index.
  ISBN 0-8242-1002-6
  1. Prisons—United States. 2. Corrections—United States. I. Herman, Peter G., 1971– II. Series

HV9471 .A46 2001
365'.973—dc21

2001045537

Visit H.W. Wilson's Web site: www.hwwilson.com

Printed in the United States of America

Contents

Preface

To appreciate the importance of incarceration in contemporary American society, one need only look at the statistics. The United States has more prisoners than any other country in the world: with approximately two million people behind bars, it holds 25 percent of the world's prisoners, though it comprises only 5 percent of the world's population. Imprisoning about 73 of every 1,000 people, the U.S. locks up a larger percentage of its population—six to 10 times more, in fact—than any other industrialized democracy. Approximately $45 billion is spent annually in the U.S. on corrections.

Such was not always the case. During the 1960s and early 1970s, there was a definite de-emphasis on incarceration in the U.S. The number of inmates in California, for example, decreased by a quarter from 1963 to 1972, despite the state's rapidly growing population. Across the country, prisons closed down. Then, partly in response to rising crime rates, prison populations began to soar in the mid-1970s. In 1973 Governor Nelson Rockefeller led the way in New York by pushing for the Rockefeller drug laws, which set strict minimum prison sentences for selling and possessing illegal drugs. Other states followed course over the next years and decades. During the 1980s and '90s the number of state prisons doubled, often spurring local economies by creating jobs.

The push to build prisons, however, could not keep pace with the skyrocketing prison population. Between 1973 and 1995 the number of people in state and federal prisons increased nearly fivefold. Prisons across the country were operating well above capacity, and the state and federal economies sagged under the cost of maintaining them. In an attempt to lower expenses, funding for many rehabilitation programs was decreased or discontinued. Meanwhile, private prison companies that charged states to hold their prisoners sprouted up across the nation, enjoying investments from Wall Street and abroad. Politicians—particularly in rural areas—who were eager to lure jobs, investment, and campaign contributions lobbied to have prisons built in their regions.

Today, according to a report by the Bureau of Justice (2000), the total number of men and women behind bars, on parole, and on probation has reached 6.3 million, more than three percent of the U.S. adult population. Most agree that this trend has come at an enormous price, not only financial, but also in terms of social costs. Have we produced a safer society by incarcerating so many individuals? Surely a murderer locked away or sentenced to death cannot murder again. Champions of the prison boom point out that the national crime rate in the 1990s has steadily decreased, dropping, for example, by seven percent between 1998 and 1999. Others argue that the reduction in crime has not been caused by increased imprisonment, but rather by an improved economy and other factors. Since the connection between crime and imprisonment is immensely complex, it is unlikely that this debate will be settled soon, nor does this book attempt to resolve such issues. Instead, it provides an extensive examination of the U.S. prison system, including the ways in which it has changed, the theories and goals of imprisonment, prison economics, race and gender issues, prison conditions, and alternatives to prison.

Section I focuses on the transformation of the American prison system, including how prisons have increasingly been brought under government oversight since the early 1900s and how prisoner rehabilitation programs initiated since that time have been scaled down. Articles in Section I vary in their focus, from a concentration on relevant statistics to an examination of the human face of the changing prison system.

Section II poses the following questions concerning America's criminal population: Who should be punished? How should they be punished? What are the goals of the penal system, and should they include, for example, making reparations to victims? In addition, a persistent theme throughout this section is the debate over how to handle the prevalence of drugs in prisons.

Section III looks at prison economics, including the finances of rehabilitation programs and the ongoing debate over private prisons. Introduced here is the frequently used term "prison-industrial complex," which Eric Schlosser, in *Atlantic Monthly* (December 1998), has described as "a set of bureaucratic, political, and economic interests that encourage increased spending on imprisonment."

A disproportionate number of African-Americans and Latinos fill American prisons—approximately 65 percent of state and federal inmates. Racial minorities account for 79 percent of all state prison drug offenders. The number of women prisoners is also growing at an alarming rate. Section IV looks at the issues of race and gender as they affect the prison system.

Because prisons are often dominated by racially determined, segregated gangs, race also comes into play in Section V, which examines prison conditions. One of the articles in this section glances behind the bars at new maximum security, or "supermax" prisons.

The book's final section examines alternative means to deterring or correcting unlawful behavior, including public shaming and what is known as "restorative justice," in which prisoners are forced to make amends to the communities, and sometimes the specific individuals, they have harmed. In addition, given the prevalence of drug offenders in prison, the use of drug rehabilitation programs as an alternative to prison is considered.

I would like to thank the authors and publications that granted permission to reprint the material contained in this volume. Thanks also to everyone at H.W. Wilson who made this book possible: Lynn Messina, Sandra Watson, Gray Young, Rich Stein, Jacquelene Latif, and Tia Brown.

Peter G. Herman
October 2001

I. Doing Time: The Transformation of American Prisons

Editor's Introduction

At the Limestone Correctional Facility in Capshaw, Alabama, prisoners shackled together with leg irons swing sledgehammers in the southern heat. Armed guards watch the repetitive rise and fall of the hammers, while the prisoners labor through the day, breaking chunks of limestone into gravel.

This scene occurred not in the 1920s but in August 1995, when Alabama became the first state to reintroduce the long-vanished chain gangs. Penal institutions in other states followed suit, embracing a form of punishment many had assumed would never be seen again in the U.S. In an odd twist, female prisoners in Arizona can *volunteer* to work on chain gangs, where they pick up litter or even bury bodies. In Texas, Indiana, Nebraska, Florida, Maine, and elsewhere, prisoners are now dressed in the striped suits of yesteryear, a practice that by the 1950s had been largely abolished by progressive administrators trying to usher in a new era of corrections.

Prevailing attitudes toward crime and punishment in America have changed countless times in the country's history, oscillating between increased tolerance and rehabilitation on the one hand, and stricter retributive penalties on the other. These changing viewpoints are reflected in our prisons—in fluctuating prison populations, changing sentencing patterns, and differing forms of treatment. Section I reviews reforms in the American prison system since the beginning of the 20th century.

In "A Century's Legacy: Five Critical Developments in the Evolution of American Prisons, 1900–2000," John W. Roberts reviews a number of improvements to the prison system made during the 20th century. The introduction of professional organizations and formalized education for prison employees has helped correctional facilities reach certain standards, Roberts notes. Other improvements include separating prison populations according to gender and graveness of offense; bringing prisons under state and federal government oversight; introducing halfway houses to aid recently released prisoners; and creating inmate programs, such as literacy classes, vocational training, and counseling. This last practice, Roberts points out, has recently been scaled back in many correctional facilities.

"The Past and Future of U.S. Prison Policy: Twenty-five Years after the Stanford Prison Experiment" focuses on changes in the prison system in the past 30 years. The psychologists Craig Haney and Philip Zimbardo recall their famous Stanford Prison Experiment of 1973, which demonstrated the deleterious effects of being a prisoner in a simulated prison. In the experiment, several psychologically healthy young men subjected to a prison environment began treating each other inhumanely. The authors note that their findings seem at odds with succeeding trends in imprisonment, where the focus has moved away from rehabilitation toward punishment.

The final two selections diverge from the theoretical into the realm of real-life experience. In "My Life As a Prison Teacher," Robert Ellis Gordon reports on cutbacks in prison educational programs and describes his teaching experiences at various prisons. Gordon's recent visit to a correctional facility reveals with disturbing immediacy the connection between violence and ignorance. Next, Sheryl Gay Stolberg, in "Behind Bars, New Effort to Care for the Dying," witnesses the effects of longer prison terms. She visits several aging inmates who will likely spend their last days behind bars.

A Century's Legacy

Five Critical Developments in the Evolution of American Prisons, 1900–2000[1]

BY JOHN W. ROBERTS
CORRECTIONS TODAY, AUGUST 2000

It was the beginning of the 20th century and leading corrections officials exhibited an almost self-congratulatory mood. "The period of barbarous treatment of prisoners . . . is passed and a new era has dawned upon us," said Rev. William Stoudenmire, general agent of the Maryland Prisoners Aid Association.

"Penology has made progress, and its only progress, in the past century," declared Superintendent Joseph Scott of the Massachusetts Reformatory. "In fact," he continued, "the whole history of prison reform is embraced in this period."

Yet, as momentous as the transformations in corrections during the 19th century were, equally momentous transformations would occur during the century that lay ahead. They were more far-reaching than the momentary philosophical arguments over the medical model or the control model. They were more profound than the mind-boggling advances in security technology. They were the fundamental changes that influenced the way corrections perceived itself and carried out its mission and they were reflected in many other reforms that occurred during 10 turbulent decades.

Professionalization

In 1900, there were many wardens, administrators, chaplains and reformers who had devoted their careers to prison management, the improvement of prison conditions and greater public understanding of prison issues. Individuals such as Robert W. McClaughry, Katherine B. Davis and Thomas Mott Osborne were corrections professionals in every sense of the term. Further, the National Prison Association (NPA)—forerunner of the American Correctional Association (ACA)—already had been in existence for three decades, providing a valuable professional forum for prison officials to meet, share ideas and advocate solutions.

---

1. Reprinted with permission of the American Correctional Association, Lanham, Md.

But the field of corrections as a whole was a long way from achieving professionalism. Then, four key developments during the 20th century combined to advance both the corrections profession and the professionalism of correctional employees.

First, organizations such as ACA and the National Institute of Corrections (NIC) established standards and provided professional authority. The formation of NPA was part of a national trend in many fields during the late 19th century to define standards and enhance professionalism. NPA adopted a declaration of principles in its inaugural year, setting goals and standards in prison work and, in 1946, it published its first Manual of Prison Standards. In 1974, ACA created the Commission on Accreditation for Corrections (CAC). The standards on which CAC bases accreditation have been extremely influential, providing benchmarks and goals even for institutions that have not been accredited. NIC, a federal agency created in 1972, has strengthened corrections professionalism further through a wide-ranging program of technical assistance, training, grants and informational services.

The formation of NPA was part of a national trend in many fields during the late 19th century to define standards and enhance professionalism.

Second, the social sciences emerged as academic disciplines in the first quarter of the 20th century. They helped provide an intellectual framework for correctional pursuits, and gave rise to the study of corrections as a specialized academic field. By the 1960s and 1970s, there were correctional programs in place at Southern Illinois University, Sam Houston State University, the University of Florida and elsewhere, which helped produce valuable scholarship on correctional issues and trained many of the profession's leaders of the 1970s, 1980s and 1990s.

Third, correctional employment was depoliticized. In 1900, most prison appointments—even for entry-level positions—were a matter of political patronage. As late as the mid-1930s, a complete staff turnover occurred at a Missouri prison in only two years because each member of the state Legislature was entitled to appoint an officer, and similar turnovers took place (albeit over slightly longer periods of time) in numerous other states. In many cases, as one observer noted, "such changes were followed inevitably by disturbances and disorganization in the service."

In 1937, all Federal Bureau of Prisons (BOP) employees except the director and assistant directors were chosen through competitive civil service procedures rather than political patronage, and that standard eventually became practically universal in major correctional agencies. Along with nonpartisan, competitive appointment came merit promotion, the establishment of correctional work as a career opportunity and even the adoption of more accurate and professional job titles—the most prominent being "officer" instead of "guard." In addition, despite the facts that the top jobs in correctional agencies continued to be political appointments and incumbents in those positions had to navigate through the shark-infested waters of state and national politics, the truly monumental figures of 20th-century corrections—James Bennett and Norman Carlson of BOP, Richard McGee of California, Austin McCormick of New York, Lovell Bixby of New Jersey, etc.—transcended politics in many respects, often serving both Republican and Democratic administrations and commanding bipartisan respect.

Fourth, staff training has undergone revolutionary changes during the past century. An incoming staff member in 1900 might have been handed a small booklet of institutional rules and regulations to memorize, but the primary form of staff training was to send new recruits to their posts with the expectation that they would pick up the rudiments of their responsibilities from the grizzled veterans who had done their jobs before. Both preservice and in-service educational qualifications and training requirements were practically nonexistent. . . .

Real advances in staff training . . . did not come until the 1970s and 1980s—not coincidentally at about the same time accreditation was being introduced and judicial oversight was increasing, and in the aftermath of several tragic inmate uprisings. Between 1972 and 1985, no fewer than two dozen state DOCs [Departments of Corrections] opened training academies. BOP opened regional training centers in the early 1970s and then consolidated basic training and other training activities in 1982 at its own section of the Federal Law Enforcement Training Center in Glynco, Ga. In the 1980s and 1990s, BOP opened several specialized training centers. Advanced training opportunities for prison officials from all jurisdictions became available in 1981, when NIC opened the National Academy of Corrections in Colorado.

Today, BOP and nearly every state DOC operate at least one training academy, which, in most cases, provides both preservice and in-service training, as well as both residential and nonresidential programs. Agencies that do not have their own academies either send staff to state police training centers or provide decentralized training programs at individual institutions. Basic training regimens last anywhere from several days to several weeks and are supplemented by in-service and annual refresher training. The range of training provided, both in the academies and in institution-based programs, is impressive: law enforcement and inmate custody procedures, investigative techniques, courtroom procedure, substance abuse issues, AIDS awareness, treatment of special needs offenders, counseling and case management, supervisory skills, ethics and media relations, as well as specialized, advanced training in everything from food service management to legal issues.

Classification and Diversified Housing

The notion of classification and diversified housing was nothing new, even in 1900. In Europe, there had been talk for centuries about segregating inmates by sex, age, severity of offense or state of mental health. There even were a few attempts, such as at Le Stinche Prison in Italy, the Spinhuis in Holland and the Brideswells in England, to do so. In the United States, early prisons in Philadelphia (Walnut Street Jail) and New York (Newgate Prison) segregated the most dangerous felons from their general populations in the 1790s, and throughout the 19th century, there were several attempts to provide separate housing for female inmates (although usually in units adjacent to or part of male prisons). The adult reformatory movement in the last quarter of the 19th century also reflected a belief that certain classes of inmates could be redeemed and would benefit from separate housing and special rehabilitative programs.

Further, classification-like grading systems were adopted in many American penitentiaries by the late 19th century. Reflecting individual inmates' institutional adjustment more than anything else, the systems typically assigned inmates to one of three grades based on their behavior and offered gradually increased or decreased privileges as they moved up or down the grade structure.

Despite the existence of grading systems, reformatories and a few separate facilities for women and juveniles, classification and diversified housing were far from a reality in 1900. Even when segregated from male inmates, women usually were confined to a corner or an attic of a men's prison. While some adult male offenders were diverted to reformatories, the vast majority of male inmates were fated to serve their sentences in fortress-like, maximum-security penitentiaries featuring Auburn-style inside cell blocks—regardless of their offenses, lengths of sentence or previous criminal records. Housing and program assignments—if they could be called that— primarily were based on what was available rather than on what was appropriate for the specific inmate.

During the first decades of the 20th century, segregation of inmates by sex and age became much more widespread. Katherine B. Davis, Mabel Walker Willebrandt, Mary B. Harris and other pioneers in the criminal justice field joined forces with politically active women's clubs to help foster a proliferation of prisons that were run for women and by women. Youth reformatories multiplied as well. By the 1950s, several states had established youth authorities to manage institutions for younger offenders and, on the federal level, BOP operated several prisons exclusively for inmates sentenced under the Federal Juvenile Delinquency Act and the Youth Corrections Act.

Having separated out the female and youthful offenders, prison authorities began dividing the majority of inmates who remained— i.e., the adult male felons—into classes. The concept of individualized treatment came into prominence among correctional scholars and officials in the 1920s and 1930s. Led by agencies such as BOP and DOCs in such states as California, New Jersey, New York, Massachusetts and Minnesota, institutions compiled a case history on each inmate and classification boards or assignment committees attempted to place inmates in the housing environment and prescribe the mix of programs that would be most conducive to rehabilitation based on each inmate's specific needs or problems. That was the guiding principle, at least. As individualized treatment evolved into the medical model by the 1960s, more sophisticated classification methods were adopted in many prison systems, including Quay Typology and the Megaree-Bohn model, which were based on the Minnesota Multiphasic Personality Inventory.

During the first decades of the 20th century, segregation of inmates by sex and age became much more widespread.

Although the classification modalities of the second and third quarters of the 20th century stressed individual psychologies and promised customized treatment programs, there were security ramifications that were equally important. It was no accident that inmates classified as "intractable" were routed to more restrictive facilities and those identified as "improvable" went to less restrictive ones.

Security concerns as part of the classification process became paramount in the 1970s and 1980s, as the medical model lost its luster and as prison systems had to cope with increasingly violent and disruptive inmates. In the late 1970s, BOP implemented its new objective classification system, designed to ensure appropriate security level designations for all inmates. By the mid-1980s, nearly every state prison system had adopted either BOP's system, one devised by NIC, the Correctional Classification Profile (which also stressed security factors) or some combination of those models. . . .

Entirely new types of prisons began appearing. Many states established reception centers or diagnostic facilities strictly for the purpose of orienting and classifying newly committed offenders. Prison hospitals, psychiatric centers and even early detoxification centers called "narcotics farms" commenced operations to serve various special needs offenders.

The "one size fits all" approach to incarceration, under which the majority of state and federal offenders served their sentences in traditional penitentiaries, was ancient history by the middle of the 20th century.

Inmate Program Opportunities

Closely connected with improvements in classification during the 20th century were improvements in programming. Starting in the 1870s, the reformatory movement had emphasized academic education, vocational training and other features commonly associated with modern program offerings, but only a minority of inmates were incarcerated in reformatories. For most inmates in 1900, program opportunities were minimal.

By 1950, however, divisions of correctional agencies, entire departments at individual correctional facilities and the careers of individual corrections professionals were devoted to programming. The programming side of corrections had attained equal stature to the previously dominant custody side. Perhaps programming even surpassed custody during the 1960s, but equilibrium was re-established by the 1980s, after the medical model had faded away. . . .

For decades, prisons throughout the United States generated additional revenue to support their operations by selling inmate-produced merchandise on the open market. By the second half of the 19th century, that process had metastasized into various strains of the offender leasing system, whereby private business interests obtained—and mercilessly exploited—the labor of inmates. The worst examples of offender leasing occurred in the South, where, for several decades, it functioned as a replacement for the institution of slavery and frequently involved compelling inmates to perform back breaking work under conditions of nearly unimaginable brutality.

On the other end of the spectrum, there were many prisons in which there were practically no constructive activities to keep inmates busy. Desperate to find something for inmates to do, wardens spread work assignments unbelievably thin. At one Ohio prison in the 1920s, an inmate was even given the task of keeping salt and pepper shakers neatly lined up on mess hall tables. Prisons were forced to resort to mind-numbing, make-work projects that were excruciating and pointless.

Further complicating matters was the legitimate concern of workers in the community that their livelihoods were being undermined by the existence of prison labor. Federal and state laws were enacted to restrict the sales of inmate-produced goods and to combat the national disgrace of convict leasing.

The answer was the state-use system. By putting inmates to work manufacturing products for sale exclusively to government agencies, prisons were better able to keep inmates occupied, while at the same time, reducing direct competition against the private sector and avoiding the exploitative character of inmate leasing. The prison systems of New Jersey, New York, Ohio and Pennsylvania spearheaded the movement to state-use production during the first quarter of the 20th century. In 1919, federal prisons began to manufacture textile products and shoes for the military. By the 1920s, nearly a dozen states had implemented the state-use system. The real landmark development, however, came in 1934, with the incorporation of Federal Prison Industries (FPl). FPI became the model state-use enterprise, with a highly diverse product line to ensure both a reliable stream of orders and a minimal impact on any one sector of the economy, as well as an ability to strengthen public support by turning to a board of directors composed of labor leaders, corporate executives and representatives of consumer and agricultural interests.

Stable work programs gave impetus to other program initiatives. Vocational training programs, for example, went hand-in-hand with work programs. Revenues generated by state-use manufacturing could be earmarked for education, recreation and other forms of inmate programming.

During the middle of the 20th century, when individualized treatment and the medical model were in vogue, programming became a primary focus of correctional administration. Classification teams assigned specific programming regimens—literacy classes, vocational training, psychological counseling, substance abuse treatment, etc.—were designed to meet the specific needs or weaknesses of individual inmates and hopefully, encourage rehabilitation. Some correctional agencies even set up research departments to monitor program effectiveness.

Programming continued to flourish even after the medical model was discarded and inmate program participation—except in work assignments—generally ceased to be mandatory. That was because most major prison systems retained offering rehabilitation opportunities to those inmates who wanted to take advantage of them as a central goal. Just as important, prison administrators recognized that any activities that reduced potentially dangerous inmate idleness could contribute significantly to better inmate management.

The emphasis on programming had another significant effect on prison operations: It was at least partly responsible for the creation of unit management. The cottage organizations of women's prisons in the early 1900s were an important precursor of unit management, but unit management did not fully come into its own until the 1970s. Dividing prisons into functional units, each with its own permanently assigned staff and a unit manager who served as a mini-warden, was undertaken largely to improve program delivery. Many units—drug treatment units, in particular—were established to focus on specific program needs. But unit management also proved to be one of the most efficient methods of inmate supervision and control, and promoted more advantageous interaction between staff and inmates. Unit management even had an impact on prison design, encouraging the movement to modular housing units and decentralized compounds.

Paradoxically, if unit management and the decentralization of operations at individual prisons was a legacy of the 20th century, so was the creation of correctional agencies and the centralization of prison systems.

Halfway Houses

Halfway houses probably were the last major component of corrections to take root, even though other elements of community corrections—probation and parole—were fairly commonplace in the early 1900s.

There were a few 19th century harbingers of halfway houses. . . .

The halfway house concept, however, lay dormant until the 1950s, when church groups founded St. Leonard's House in Chicago, Dismas House in St. Louis and Crenshaw House in Los Angeles. By that time, several prisons had introduced prerelease units within their walls to prepare inmates to return to the community as their discharge dates approached.

The real breakthrough for halfway houses came in 1961, when, at the request of BOP Director James Bennett, U.S. Attorney General Robert F. Kennedy directed BOP to establish pilot "prerelease guidance centers" in several cities, where youthful offenders could live while working in the community during the last months of their incarceration. Not only did these centers offer shelter and help younger offenders get started in honest employment, they also provided ongoing supervision during the transition from prison to freedom, offered wholesome recreational activities, provided counseling and arranged for lectures and classes on everything from seeking jobs to finding apartments and mastering social skills. The prerelease guidance centers proved to be such an unqualified success that halfway houses—called community treatment centers—were made available under the 1965 Federal Prisoner Rehabilitation Act for BOP's adult inmates. The community treatment centers worked so well there was even talk that they might play a role in "decarceration," i.e., the virtual emptying of the nation's prisons. Indeed, the federal prison population actually began to drop in the late 1960s as the halfway house population grew.

Decarceration, of course, never took hold. But the success of the federal halfway house program inspired a wave of halfway house development by state and city correctional agencies across the country. The trend was encouraged further by the establishment in 1964 of the International Halfway House Association.

By the end of the 20th century, halfway houses—which were practically unknown in 1900—were an indispensable part of corrections. Hundreds of halfway houses, community treatment facilities and community corrections centers were being operated, either directly by DOCs or on a contract basis by private organizations such as Volunteers of America, the Salvation Army and Goodwill Industries. Moreover, the role of halfway houses had expanded to include, in addition to prerelease cases, pretrial defendants, individuals on probation, probation violators, direct court commitments and even expectant and new mothers serving sentences, so that they could give birth and spend a few months with their babies outside prison settings.

> *By the end of the 20th century, halfway houses—which were practically unknown in 1900—were an indispensable part of corrections.*

Rules, Authority and Judicial Oversight

Individual prisons in 1900 operated almost autonomously and prison wardens exercised almost absolute power. Many prisons issued rules and regulations, but they hardly were exhaustive. Much discretion was left to individual staff members on how to deal with inmates and to wardens on how to manage institutions. Once an offender was lawfully committed to a prison, he or she virtually was at the mercy of prison staff, with little recourse in the event of misunderstandings or abuse. . . .

From the 1880s through the early 1900s, modest progress toward increased centralization took place as many states—with Kansas, Massachusetts, Minnesota and New York in the lead—began consolidating the various boards of trustees that existed for individual prisons into single boards or prison commissions that would oversee correctional operations statewide. It was not until the 1930s and

1940s, however, that state legislatures created DOCs, the U.S. Congress created BOP and permanent bureaucratic structures were put in place to administer prison operations on a day-to-day basis. Along with these new bureaucratic structures came codifications of rules, regulations and procedures, spelling out in great detail exactly how prisons would operate, how staff would conduct themselves and how inmates would be treated. Slender and easily disregarded rule books grew into imposing, multivolume manuals that might be disdained, but could only be disregarded at an officer's or a warden's peril.

Old-line wardens resisted at first, but centralization of administration and codification of regulations was a vital stage in the maturation process of America's prisons. Without clearly articulated regulations and policies, and without agency directors who had the muscle to carry them out, the reforms of the individualized treatment era would never have been realized. They also made it possible for prisons to operate in a rational, interrelated basis, with each institution in a prison system performing a specific mission while adhering to agencywide standards and consistent patterns of administration. Creation of DOCs also fostered a career service by providing more opportunities both for training and promotion. Finally, centralized administration and codification of regulations ensured greater recognition of inmate rights—perhaps the most significant legacy of 20th-century corrections.

Equally important, courts began to take a greater interest in prison operations than ever before. Until the 1960s, courts accepted the 1871 Supreme Court ruling that inmates were merely "slaves of the state," and demonstrated scant inclination to supervise or interfere with prison operations. The civil rights movement, the efforts of inmate advocacy groups and the public's revulsion with the conditions that led to riots in Attica and elsewhere helped prompt the courts to pay greater attention to life behind prison walls. As the Supreme Court stated in 1974, there was "no iron curtain drawn between the Constitution and the prisons of this country."

Since the late 1960s, tens of thousands of individual and class action lawsuits have been filed against prisons and prison administrators. Enough of them had sufficient merit to warrant widespread and intensive judicial intervention, up to and including the court-ordered restructuring of an entire state prison system.

Checks and balances, long an afterthought in American corrections, had moved to center stage by the last quarter of the 20th century.

And Yet . . .

Despite the advances in corrections, the last years of the 20th century witnessed a number of well-publicized retreats to the past. Such relics as chain gangs and striped uniforms were resuscitated, boot camps recalled the military drills of the reformatory era, parole was cut back to 19th-century levels in many jurisdictions and corrections was thrust back into the partisan arena to become as much of a political football as any time in its history. As Alexander Pisciotta wisely pointed out in his reassessment of Brockway, the "march of progress" approach to correctional history tends to obscure unresolved challenges, failed efforts and enduring problems. Even the most cursory examination of the proceedings of early 20th-century NPA congresses and the memoirs of Sanford Bates, McGee, Bennett, Harris and others suggests that the issues and concerns with which corrections officials grappled in years past—security imperatives, the debate of punishment vs. rehabilitation, special needs offenders and the wildly distorted public perceptions of corrections—were not much different from those facing corrections officials today.

> *Despite the advances in corrections, the last years of the 20th century witnessed a number of well-publicized retreats to the past.*

The timeless dilemmas, however, do not diminish the fact that corrections has evolved during the past 100 years—significantly and for the better. The 20th-century trends toward greater professionalism, establishment of classification and diversified housing, enhancements in programming, more extensive reliance on community corrections, centralization of authority and codification of rules, have resulted in better-qualified staff, improved conditions of confinement, more effective management and a greater ability on the part of corrections to carry out its public missions.

References

Bates, S. (1971). *Prisons and beyond.* (Reprint edition.) Freeport, N.Y.: Books for Libraries Press.

Dilulio, J. J., Jr. (1987). *Governing prisons: A comparative study of correctional management.* New York: Free Press.

Keve, P. W. (1999). Building a better prison: The first three decades of the Detroit House of Correction. *Michigan Historical Review,* 25(3): 1–28.

Keve, P. W. (1995). *Measuring excellence: The history of correctional standards and accreditation.* Lanham, Md.: American Correctional Association.

Keve, P. W. (1991). *Prisons and the American conscience: A History of U.S. federal corrections.* Carbondale, Ill.: Southern Illinois University Press.

Levinson, R. B. (1994). The development of classification and programming. In *Escaping prison myths: Selected topics in the history of federal corrections,* ed. John W. Roberts, 95–110. Washington, D.C.: American University Press.

McCarthy, B. R., & McCarthy, B. J., Jr. (1991). *Community-based corrections, second edition.* Pacific Grove, Calif.: Brooks/Cole Publishing Co.

McKelvey, B. (1977). *American prisons: A history of good intentions, reprint edition.* Montclair, N.J.: Patterson Smith.

McShane, M. D., & Williams, F. P. III. (1996). *Encyclopedia of American prisons.* New York: Garland Publishing.

National Prison Association. (1901). *National prison congress proceedings.* Pittsburgh: Shaw Brothers.

National Prison Association. (1902). *National prison congress proceedings.* Pittsburgh: Shaw Brothers.

Pisciotta, A. (1994). *Benevolent repression: Social control and the American reformatory movement.* New York: New York University Press.

Robbins, I. P. (1994). The prisoner's mail box and the evolution of federal inmate rights. In *Escaping prison myths: Selected topics in the history of federal corrections,* ed. John W. Roberts, 111–158. Washington, D.C.: American University Press.

Van Voorhis, P. (1994). *Psychological classification of the adult male prison inmate.* Albany, N.Y.: SUNY Press.

The Past and Future of U.S. Prison Policy

Twenty-five Years after the Stanford Prison Experiment[2]

By Craig Haney and Philip Zimbardo
American Psychologist, July 1998

Twenty-five years ago, a group of psychologically healthy, normal college students (and several presumably mentally sound experimenters) were temporarily but dramatically transformed in the course of six days spent in a prison-like environment, in research that came to be known as the Stanford Prison Experiment (SPE; Haney, Banks, & Zimbardo, 1973). The outcome of our study was shocking and unexpected to us, our professional colleagues, and the general public. Otherwise emotionally strong college students who were randomly assigned to be mock-prisoners suffered acute psychological trauma and breakdowns. Some of the students begged to be released from the intense pains of less than a week of merely simulated imprisonment, whereas others adapted by becoming blindly obedient to the unjust authority of the guards. The guards, too—who also had been carefully chosen on the basis of their normal-average scores on a variety of personality measures—quickly internalized their randomly assigned role. Many of these seemingly gentle and caring young men, some of whom had described themselves as pacifists or Vietnam War "doves," soon began mistreating their peers and were indifferent to the obvious suffering that their actions produced. Several of them devised sadistically inventive ways to harass and degrade the prisoners, and none of the less actively cruel mock-guards ever intervened or complained about the abuses they witnessed. Most of the worst prisoner treatment came on the night shifts and other occasions when the guards thought they could avoid the surveillance and interference of the research team. Our planned two-week experiment had to be aborted after only six days because the experience dramatically and painfully transformed most of the participants in ways we did not anticipate, prepare for, or predict.

---

2. Article by Craig Haney and Philip Zimbardo from *American Psychologist* July 1998, vol. 53, no. 7, pp. 709–727. Copyright © 1998 American Psychological Association. Reprinted with permission.

These shocking results attracted an enormous amount of public and media attention and became the focus of much academic writing and commentary. For example, in addition to our own analyses of the outcome of the study itself (e.g., Haney et al., 1973; Haney & Zimbardo, 1977; Zimbardo, 1975; Zimbardo, Haney, Banks, & Jaffe, 1974) and the various methodological and ethical issues that it raised (e.g., Haney, 1976; Zimbardo, 1973), the SPE was hailed by former American Psychological Association president George Miller (1980) as an exemplar of the way in which psychological research could and should be "given away" to the public because its important lessons could be readily understood and appreciated by nonprofessionals. On the 25th anniversary of this study, we reflect on its continuing message for contemporary prison policy in light of the quarter century of criminal justice history that has transpired since we concluded the experiment.

Our study represented an experimental demonstration of the extraordinary power of institutional environments to influence those who passed through them.

When we conceived of the SPE, the discipline of psychology was in the midst of what has been called a "situational revolution." Our study was one of the "host of celebrated laboratory and field studies" that Ross and Nisbett (1991) referred to as having demonstrated the ways in which "the immediate social situation can overwhelm in importance the type of individual differences in personal traits or dispositions that people normally think of as being determinative of social behavior" (p. xiv). Along with much other research conducted over the past two and one-half decades illustrating the enormous power of situations, the SPE is often cited in textbooks and journal articles as a demonstration of the way in which social contexts can influence, alter, shape, and transform human behavior.

Our goal in conducting the SPE was to extend that basic perspective—one emphasizing the potency of social situations—into a relatively unexplored area of social psychology. Specifically, our study represented an experimental demonstration of the extraordinary power of *institutional* environments to influence those who passed through them. In contrast to the companion research of Stanley Milgram (1974) that focused on individual compliance in the face of an authority figure's increasingly extreme and unjust demands, the SPE examined the conformity pressures brought to bear on groups of people functioning within the same institutional setting (see

Carr, 1995). Our "institution" rapidly developed sufficient power to bend and twist human behavior in ways that confounded expert predictions and violated the expectations of those who created and participated in it. And, because the unique design of the study allowed us to minimize the role of personality or dispositional variables, the SPE yielded especially clear psychological insights about the nature and dynamics of social and institutional control.

The behavior of prisoners and guards in our simulated environment bore a remarkable similarity to patterns found in actual prisons. As we wrote, "Despite the fact that guards and prisoners were essentially free to engage in any form of interaction . . . the characteristic nature of their encounters tended to be negative, hostile, affrontive and dehumanising" (Haney et al., 1973, p. 80). Specifically, verbal interactions were pervaded by threats, insults, and deindividuating references that were most commonly directed by guards against prisoners. The environment we had fashioned in the basement hallway of Stanford University's Department of Psychology became so real for the participants that it completely dominated their day-to-day existence (e.g., 90% of prisoners' incell conversations focused on "prison"-related topics), dramatically affected their moods and emotional states (e.g., prisoners expressed three times as much negative affect as did guards), and at least temporarily undermined their sense of self (e.g., both groups expressed increasingly more deprecating self-evaluations over time). Behaviorally, guards most often gave commands and engaged in confrontive or aggressive acts toward prisoners, whereas the prisoners initiated increasingly less behavior; failed to support each other more often than not; negatively evaluated each other in ways that were consistent with the guards' views of them; and as the experiment progressed, more frequently expressed intentions to do harm to others (even as they became increasingly more docile and conforming to the whims of the guards). We concluded,

> The negative, anti-social reactions observed were not the product of an environment created by combining a collection of deviant personalities, but rather the result of an intrinsically pathological situation which could distort and rechannel the behaviour of essentially normal individuals. The abnormality here resided in the psychological nature of the situation and not in those who passed through it. (Haney et al., 1973, p. 90)

In much of the research and writing we have done since then, the SPE has served as an inspiration and intellectual platform from which to extend the conceptual relevance of situational variables into two very different domains. One of us examined the coercive power of legal institutions in general and prisons in particular (e.g., Haney, 1993a, 1997b, 1997c, 1997d, 1998; Haney & Lynch, 1997), as well as the importance of situational factors in explaining and reducing crime (e.g., Haney, 1983, 1994, 1995, 1997a). The other of us explored the dimensions of intrapsychic "psychological prisons" that constrict human experience and undermine human potential (e.g., Brodt & Zimbardo, 1981; Zimbardo, 1977; Zimbardo, Pilkonis, & Norwood, 1975) and the ways in which "mind-altering" social psychological dynamics can distort individual judgment and negatively influence behavior (e.g., Zimbardo, 1979a; Zimbardo & Andersen, 1993). Because the SPE was intended as a critical demonstration of the negative effects of extreme institutional environments, much of the work that grew out of this original study was change-oriented and explored the ways in which social and legal institutions and practices might be transformed to make them more responsive to humane psychological imperatives (e.g., Haney, 1993b; Haney & Pettigrew, 1986; Haney & Zimbardo, 1977; Zimbardo, 1975; Zimbardo et al., 1974).

In this article, we return to the core issue that guided the original study (Haney et al., 1973)—the implications of situational models of behavior for criminal justice institutions. We use the SPE as a point of historical departure to briefly examine the ways in which policies concerning crime and punishment have been transformed over the intervening 25 years. We argue that a series of psychological insights derived from the SPE and related studies, and the broad perspective that they advanced, still can contribute to the resolution of many of the critical problems that currently plague correctional policy in the United States.

Crime and Punishment a Quarter Century Ago

The story of how the nature and purpose of imprisonment have been transformed over the past 25 years is very different from the one that we once hoped and expected we would be able to tell. At the time we conducted the SPE—in 1971—there was widespread concern about the fairness and the efficacy of the criminal justice system. Scholars, politicians, and members of the public wondered aloud whether prisons were too harsh, whether they adequately rehabilitated prisoners, and whether there were alternatives to incarceration that would better serve correctional needs and interests. Many states were already alarmed about increased levels of overcrowding. Indeed, in those days, prisons that operated at close to 90% of capacity were thought to be dangerously overcrowded. It was widely understood by legislators and penologists alike that under such conditions, programming resources were stretched too thin, and prison administrators were left with increasingly fewer degrees of freedom with which to respond to interpersonal conflicts and a range of other inmate problems.

Despite these concerns about overcrowding, there was a functional moratorium on prison construction in place in most parts of the country. Whatever else it represented, the moratorium reflected a genuine skepticism at some of the very highest levels of government about the viability of prison as a solution to the crime problem. Indeed, the report of the National Advisory Commission on Criminal Justice Standards and Goals (1973), published at around the same time we published the results of the SPE, concluded that prisons, juvenile reformatories, and jails had achieved what it characterized as a "shocking record of failure" (p. 597), suggested that these institutions may have been responsible for creating more crime than they prevented, and recommended that the moratorium on prison construction last at least another 10 years.

> *There was a functional moratorium on prison construction in place in most parts of the country.*

To be sure, there was a fiscal undercurrent to otherwise humanitarian attempts to avoid the overuse of imprisonment. Prisons are expensive, and without clear evidence that they worked very well, it was difficult to justify building and running more of them (cf. Scull, 1977). But there was also a fair amount of genuine concern among the general public about what was being done to prisoners behind prison walls and what the long-term effects would be (e.g., Mitford, 1973; Yee, 1973). The SPE and its attendant publicity added to that skepticism, but the real challenge came from other deeper currents in the larger society.

The late 1960s saw the beginning of a prisoners' rights movement that eventually raised the political consciousness of large numbers of prisoners, some of whom became effective spokespersons for their cause (e.g., American Friends Service Committee, 1971; Jackson, 1970; Smith, 1993). Widely publicized, tragic events in several prisons in different parts of the country vividly illustrated how prisoners could be badly mistreated by prison authorities and underscored the potentially serious drawbacks of relying on prisons as the centerpiece in a national strategy of crime control. For example, just a few weeks after the SPE was concluded, prisoners in Attica, New York, held a number of correctional officers hostage in a vain effort to secure more humane treatment. Although national celebrities attempted to peaceably mediate the standoff, an armed assault to retake the prison ended tragically with the deaths of many hostages and prisoners. Subsequent revelations about the use of excessive force and an official cover-up contributed to public skepticism about prisons and doubts about the wisdom and integrity of some of their administrators (e.g., Wicker, 1975).

Legal developments also helped to shape the prevailing national Zeitgeist on crime and punishment. More than a decade before we conducted the SPE, the U.S. Supreme Court had defined the Eighth Amendment's ban on cruel and unusual punishment as one that drew its meaning from what Chief Justice Warren called "the evolving standards of decency that mark the progress of a maturing society" *(Trop v. Dulles,* 1958, p. 101). It is probably fair to say that most academics, and other informed citizens anticipated that these standards *were* evolving and in such a way that the institution of prison—as the major organ of state-sanctioned punishment in American society—would be scrutinized carefully and honestly in an effort to apply contemporary humane views, including those that were emerging from the discipline of psychology.

Psychologists Stanley Brodsky, Carl Clements, and Raymond Fowler were engaged in just such a legal effort to reform the Alabama prison system in the early 1970s *(Pugh v. Locke,* 1976; Yackle, 1989). The optimism with which Fowler (1976) wrote about the results of that litigation was characteristic of the time: "The practice of psychology in the nation's correctional systems, long a neglected byway, could gain new significance and visibility as a result [of the court's ruling]" (p. 15). The same sentiments prevailed in a similar effort in which we participated along with psychologist Thomas Hilliard (1976) in litigation that was designed to improve conditions in a special solitary confinement unit at San Quentin (*Spain v. Procunier,* 1976). Along with other psychologists interested in correctional and legal reform, we were confident that psychology and other social scientific disciplines could be put to effective use in the creation and application of evolving standards inside the nation's prisons (see Haney & Zimbardo, 1977).

And then, almost without warning, all of this critical reappraisal and constructive optimism about humane standards and alternatives to incarceration was replaced with something else. The counterrevolution in crime and punishment began slowly and imperceptibly at first and then pushed forward with a consistency of direction and effect that could not be overlooked. It moved so forcefully and seemingly inexorably during the 1980s that it resembled nothing so much as a runaway punishment train, driven by political steam and fueled by media-induced fears of crime. Now, many years after the SPE and that early optimism about psychologically based prison reform, our nation finds itself in the midst of arguably the worst corrections crisis in U.S. history, with every indication that it will get worse before it can possibly get better. For the first time in the 200-year history of imprisonment in the United States, there appear to be no limits on the amount of prison pain the public is willing to inflict in the name of crime control (cf. Haney, 1997b, 1998). Retired judge Lois Forer (1994), in her denunciation of some of these recent trends, warned of the dire consequences of what she called the "rage to punish." But this rage has been indulged so completely that it threatens to override any of the competing concerns for humane justice that once served to make this system more compassionate and fair. The United States has entered what another commentator called the "mean season" of corrections, one in which penal philosophy amounts to little more than devising "creative strategies to make offenders suffer" (Cullen, 1995, p. 340).

The Radical Transformation of "Corrections"

We briefly recount the series of wrenching transformations that laid the groundwork for the mean season of corrections that the nation has now entered—the some 25 years of correctional policy

> *Almost overnight, the concept that had served as the intellectual cornerstone of corrections policy for nearly a century—rehabilitation—was publicly and politically discredited.*

that have transpired since the SPE was conducted. Whatever the social and political forces that caused these transformations, they collectively altered the correctional landscape of the country. The criminal justice system not only has become increasingly harsh and punitive but also has obscured many of the psychological insights on which the SPE and numerous other empirical studies were based— insights about the power of social situations and contexts to influence and control behavior. Specifically, over a very short period of time, the following series of transformations occurred to radically change the shape and direction of corrections in the United States.

The Death of Rehabilitation

A dramatic shift in correctional philosophy was pivotal to the series of changes that followed. Almost overnight, the concept that had served as the intellectual cornerstone of corrections policy for nearly a century—rehabilitation—was publicly and politically discredited. The country moved abruptly in the mid-1970s from a society that justified putting people in prison on the basis of the belief that their incarceration would somehow facilitate their productive reentry into the free world to one that used imprisonment merely to disable criminal offenders ("incapacitation") or to keep them far away from the rest of society ("containment"). At a more philosophical level, imprisonment was now said to further something called "just desserts"—locking people up for no other reason than they deserved it and for no other purpose than to punish them (e.g., von Hirsch, 1976). In fact, prison punishment soon came to be thought of as its own reward, serving only the goal of inflicting pain.

Determinate Sentencing and the Politicizing of Prison Pain

Almost simultaneously—and, in essence, as a consequence of the abandonment of rehabilitation—many states moved from indeterminate to determinate models of prison sentencing. Because indeterminate sentencing had been devised as a mechanism to allow for the release of prisoners who were rehabilitated early—and the retention of those whose in-prison change took longer—it simply did not fit with the new goals of incarceration. This shift to determinate sentencing did have the intended consequence of removing discretion from the hands of prison administrators and even judges who, studies showed, from time to time abused it (e.g., American Friends Service Committee, 1971). However, it also had the likely unintended consequence of bringing prison sentencing into an openly political arena. Once largely the province of presumably expert judicial decision makers, prison administrators, or parole authorities who operated largely out of the public view, prison sentencing had remained relatively free from at least the most obvious and explicit forms of political influence. They no longer were. Moreover, determinate sentencing and the use of rigid sentencing guidelines or "grids" undermined the role of situation and context in the allocation of punishment (cf. Freed, 1992).

The Imprisoning of America

The moratorium on new prison construction that was in place at the time of the SPE was ended by the confluence of several separate, powerful forces. For one, legislators continued to vie for the mantle of "toughest on crime" by regularly increasing the lengths of prison sentences. Of course, this meant that prisoners were incarcerated for progressively longer periods of time. In addition, the sentencing discretion of judges was almost completely subjugated to the various aforementioned legislative grids, formulas, and guidelines. Moreover, the advent of determinate sentencing meant that prison administrators had no outlets at the other end of this flow of prisoners to relieve population pressures (which, under indeterminate sentencing, had been discretionary). Finally, federal district court judges began to enter judicial orders that prohibited states from, among other things, cramming two and three or more prisoners into one-person (typically six feet by nine feet) cells (e.g., *Burks v. Walsh,* 1978; *Capps v. Atiyeh,* 1980). Eventually even long-time opponents of new prisons agreed that prisoners could no longer be housed in these shockingly inadequate spaces and reluctantly faced the inevitable: Prison construction began on an unprecedented scale across the country.

Although this rapid prison construction briefly eased the over-crowding problem, prisoner populations continued to grow at unprecedented rates. It soon became clear that even dramatic increases in the number of new prisons could not keep pace. In fact, almost continuously over the past 25 years, penologists have described U.S. prisons as "in crisis" and have characterized each new level of overcrowding as "unprecedented." As the decade of the 1980s came to a close, the United States was imprisoning more people for longer periods of time than ever before in our history, far surpassing other industrialized democracies in the use of incarceration as a crime control measure (Mauer, 1992, 1995). As of June 1997, the most recent date for which figures are available, the total number of persons incarcerated in the United States exceeded 1.7 million (Bureau of Justice Statistics, 1998), which continues the upward trend of the previous 11 years, from 1985 to 1996, when the number rose from 744,208 to 1,630,940. Indeed, 10 years ago, long before today's record rates were attained, one scholar concluded, "It is easily demonstrable that America's use of prison is excessive to the point of barbarity, with a prison rate several times higher than that of other similarly developed Western countries" (Newman, 1988, p. 346). A year later, a reviewer wrote in the pages of *Contemporary Psychology*:

> American prison and jail populations have reached historically high levels. . . . It is noteworthy that, although in several recent years the levels of reported crime declined, the prison and jail populations continued to rise. The desire for punishment seems to have taken on a life of its own. (McConville, 1989, p. 928)

The push to higher rates and lengths of incarceration has only intensified since then. Most state and federal prisons now operate well above their rated capacities, with many overcrowded to nearly twice their design limits. At the start of the 1990s, the United States incarcerated more persons per capita than any other modem nation in the world. The international disparities are most striking when the U.S. incarceration rate is contrasted to those of other nations with which the United States is often compared, such as Japan, The Netherlands, Australia, and the United Kingdom; throughout most of the present decade, the U.S. rates have consistently been between four and eight times as high as those of these other nations (e.g., Christie, 1994; Mauer, 1992, 1995). In fact, rates of incarceration have continued to climb in the United States, reaching the unprecedented levels of more than 500 per 100,000 in 1992 and then 600 per 100,000 in 1996. Although in 1990 the United States incarcerated a higher proportion of its population than any other nation on earth (Mauer, 1992), as of 1995, political and economic upheaval in Russia was associated with an abrupt increase in rate of incarceration, and Russia surpassed the United States. . . .

The increase in U.S. prison populations during these years was not produced by a disproportionate increase in the incarceration of violent offenders. In 1995, only one quarter of persons sentenced to state prisons were convicted of a violent offense, whereas three quarters were sent for property or drug offenses or other nonviolent crimes such as receiving stolen property or immigration violations (Bureau of Justice Statistics, 1996). Nor was the increased use of imprisonment related to increased levels of crime. In fact, according to the National Crime Victimization Survey, conducted by the Bureau of the Census, a survey of 94,000 U.S. residents found that many fewer of them were the victims of crime during the calendar year 1995–1996, the year our incarceration rate reached an all-time high (Bureau of Justice Statistics, 1997b).

> *The United States incarcerates African-American men at a rate that is approximately four times the rate of incarceration of Black men in South Africa.*

The Racialization of Prison Pain

The aggregate statistics describing the extraordinary punitiveness of the U.S. criminal justice system mask an important fact: The pains of imprisonment have been inflicted disproportionately on minorities, especially Black men. Indeed, for many years, the rate of incarceration of White men in the United States compared favorably with those in most Western European nations, including countries regarded as the most progressive and least punitive (e.g., Dunbaugh, 1979). Although in recent years the rate of incarceration for Whites in the United States has also increased and no longer compares favorably with other Western European nations, it still does not begin to approximate the rate for African-Americans. Thus, although they represent less than 6% of the general U.S. population, African-American men constitute 48% of those confined to state prisons. Statistics collected at the beginning of this decade indicated that Blacks were more than six times more likely to be imprisoned than their White counterparts (Mauer, 1992). By 1995, that disproportion had grown to seven and one-half times (Bureau of Justice Statistics, 1996). In fact, the United States incarcerates African-American men at a rate that is approximately four times the rate of incarceration of Black men in South Africa (King, 1993).

All races and ethnic groups and both sexes are being negatively affected by the increases in the incarcerated population, but the racial comparisons are most telling. The rate of incarceration for White men almost doubled between 1985 and 1995, growing from a rate of 528 per 100,000 in 1985 to a rate of 919 per 100,000 in 1995. The impact of incarceration on African-American men, Hispanics, and women of all racial and ethnic groups is greater than that for White men, with African-American men being the most profoundly affected. The number of African-American men who are incarcerated rose from a rate of 3,544 per 100,000 in 1985 to an astonishing rate of 6,926 per 100,000 in 1995. Also, between 1985 and 1995, the number of Hispanic prisoners rose by an average of 12% annually (Mumola & Beck, 1997). . . .

The Overincarceration of Drug Offenders

The increasingly disproportionate number of African-American men who are being sent to prison seems to be related to the dramatic increase in the number of persons incarcerated for drug-related offenses, combined with the greater tendency to imprison Black drug offenders as compared with their White counterparts. Thus, although Blacks and Whites use drugs at approximately the same rate (Bureau of Justice Statistics, 1991), African-Americans were arrested for drug offenses during the so-called war on drugs at a much higher rate than were Whites (Blumstein, 1993). The most recent data show that between 1985 and 1995, the number of African-Americans incarcerated in state prisons due to drug violations (which were their only or their most serious offense) rose 707% [see Change in Estimated Number of Sentenced Prisoners, by Most Serious Offense and race, Between 1985 and 1995, on p.28]. In contrast, the number of Whites incarcerated in state prisons for drug offenses (as their only or most serious offense) underwent a 306% change. In 1986, for example, only 7% of Black prison inmates in the United States had been convicted of drug crimes, compared with 8% of Whites. By 1991, however, the Black percentage had more than tripled to 25%, whereas the percentage of White inmates incarcerated for drug crimes had increased by only half to 12% (Tonry, 1995). In the federal prison system, the numbers of African-Americans incarcerated for drug violations are shockingly high: Fully 64% of male and 71% of female Black prisoners incarcerated in federal institutions in 1995 had been sent there for drug offenses (Bureau of Justice Statistics, 1996).

According to a historical report done for the Bureau of Justice Statistics (Cahalan, 1986), the offense distribution of federal and state prisoners—a measure of the types of crimes for which people are incarcerated—remained stable from 1910 to 1984. The classification of some offenses changed. For example, robbery is now included in the category of violent crime rather than being classified with property crimes, as it was in the past. Public order offenses, also called morals charges, used to include vagrancy, liquor law violations, and drug offenses. Drug offenses are no longer classified with public order crimes. Of course, not only have drug offenses been elevated to the status of their own crime category in national statistical compilations and their own especially severe legislated penalties, but there is also a "Drug Czar" in the executive branch and a large federal agency devoted exclusively to enforcing laws against drug-related crimes.

As we noted, the types and proportions of offenses for which people were incarcerated in the United States were highly consistent for the 75 years prior to 1984. For most of the 20th century, the U.S. prison population consisted of around 60–70% offenders against property, 13–24% offenders against persons (now called violent crime), around 20% public order-morals violations (which included drug offenses), and 10% other types of offenders (Cahalan, 1986).

Change in Estimated Number of Sentenced Prisoners, by Most Serious Offense and Race, between 1985 and 1995.

Most serious offense	Total % change, 1983-1995	White % change, 1985-1995	Black % change, 1985-1995
Total	119	109	132
Violent offenses	86	92	83
Property offenses	69	74	65
Drug offenses	478	306	707
Public-order offenses [a]	187	162	229
Other/unspecified [b]	-6	-72	64

Note: Adopted from *Prisoners in 1996* (Bureau of Justice Statistics Bulletin NCJ 164619, p. 10), by C. J. Mumola and A. J. Beck, 1997, Rockville, MD: Bureau of Justice Statistics. In the public domain.

[a] Includes weapons, drunk driving, escape, court offenses, obstruction, commercialized vice, morals and decency charges, liquor law violations, and other public-order offenses.

[b] Includes juvenile offenses and unspecified felonies.

However, these distributions have changed dramatically during the past 10 to 15 years. The federal government is now willing to incarcerate people for a wider range of criminal violations, and both state and federal prisoners remain incarcerated for longer periods of time. The number of violent offenders who are incarcerated has risen but not as steeply as the number of drug offenders who are now sent to prison. In 1995, 23% of state prisoners were incarcerated for drug offenses in contrast to 9% of drug offenders in state prisons in 1986. In fact, the proportion of drug offenders in the state prison population nearly tripled by 1990, when it reached 21%, and has remained at close to that level since then. The proportion of federal prisoners held for drug violations doubled during the past 10 years. In 1985, 34% of federal prisoners were incarcerated for drug violations. By 1995, the proportion had risen to 60% [See Distribution of Offenses: State and Federal Prisons, 1985 and 1995, below].

We note in passing that these three interrelated trends—the extraordinary increase in the numbers of persons in prison, the disproportionate incarceration of minorities, and the high percentage of persons incarcerated for drug offenses—reflect a consistent disregard of context and situation in the criminal justice policies of the past 25 years. The unprecedented use of imprisonment per se manifests a policy choice to incarcerate individual lawbreakers instead of targeting the criminogenic social conditions and risk factors that have contributed to their criminality. Sentencing models that ignore

Distribution of Offenses: State and Federal Prisons, 1985 and 1995

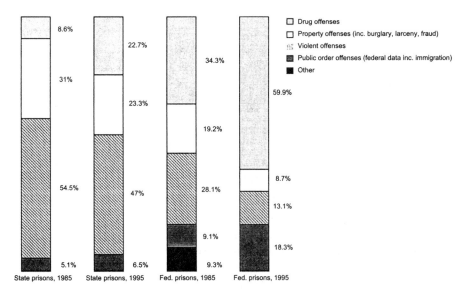

Note: Fed = federal; inc. = including

situation and context inevitably lead to higher rates of incarceration among groups of citizens who confront race-based poverty and deprivation and other social ills that are related to discrimination. The failure to address the differential opportunity structure that leads young minority group members into certain kinds of drug-related activities and the conscious decision to target those activities for criminal prosecution and incarceration, rather than to attempt to improve the life chances of the urban Black underclass, reflect dispositional—and discriminatory—views of crime control.

Moreover, excessive and disproportionate use of imprisonment ignores the secondary effects that harsh criminal justice policies eventually will have on the social contexts and communities from which minority citizens come. Remarkably, as the present decade began, there were more young Black men (between the ages of 20 and 29) under the control of the nation's criminal justice system (including probation and parole supervision) than the total number in college (Mauer, 1990). Thus, one scholar has predicted that "imprisonment will become the most significant factor contributing to the dissolution and breakdown of African-American families during the decade of the 1990s." (King, 1993, p. 145), and another has concluded that "crime control policies are a major contributor to the disruption of the family, the prevalence of single parent families, and children raised without a father in the ghetto, and the 'inability of people to get the jobs still available'" (Chambliss, 1994, p. 183).

The Rise of the "Supermax" Prison

In addition to becoming dangerously overcrowded and populated by a disproportionate number of minority citizens and drug offenders over the past 25 years, many U.S. prisons also now lack meaningful work, training, education, treatment, and counseling programs for the prisoners who are confined in them. Plagued by increasingly intolerable living conditions where prisoners serve long sentences that they now have no hope of having reduced through "good time" credits, due to laws imposed by state legislatures, many prison officials have turned to punitive policies of within-prison segregation in the hope of maintaining institutional control (e.g., Christie, 1994; Haney, 1993a; Haney & Lynch, 1997; Perkinson, 1994). Indeed, a penal philosophy of sorts has emerged in which prison systems use long-term solitary confinement in so-called supermax prisons as a proactive policy of inmate management. Criticized as the "Marionization" of U.S. prisons, after the notorious federal penitentiary in Marion, Illinois, where the policy seems to have originated (Amnesty International, 1987; Olivero & Roberts, 1990), one commentator referred to the "accelerating movement toward housing prisoners officially categorized as violent or disruptive in separate, free-standing facilities where they are locked in their cells approximately 23 hours per day" (Immarigeon, 1992, p. 1). They are ineligible for prison jobs, vocational training programs, and, in many states, education.

Thus, in the 25 years since the SPE was conducted, the country has witnessed the emergence of a genuinely new penal form—supermax prisons that feature state-of-the-art, ultra secure, long-term segregated confinement supposedly reserved for the criminal justice system's most troublesome or incorrigible offenders. Human Rights Watch (1997) described the basic routine imposed in such units: Prisoners "are removed from general population and housed in conditions of extreme social isolation, limited environmental stimulation, reduced privileges and service, scant recreational, vocational or educational opportunities, and extraordinary control over their every movement" (p. 14). (See also Haney, 1993a, 1997d, and Haney and Lynch, 1997, for discussions of the psychological effects of these special conditions of confinement.) By 1991, these prisons imposing extreme segregation and isolation were functioning in some 36 states, with many others in the planning stages (e.g., "Editorial," 1991). A newly opened, highly restrictive, modem "control unit" apparently committed the federal penitentiary system to the use of this penal form for some time to come (Dowker & Good, 1992; Perkinson, 1994). Thus, by 1997 Human Rights Watch expressed concern over what it called "the national trend toward supermaximum security prisons" (p. 13), noting that in addition to the 57 units currently in operation, construction programs already underway "would increase the nationwide supermax capacity by nearly 25 percent" (p. 14).

A constitutional challenge to conditions in California's supermax—one that many legal observers viewed as a test case on the constitutionality of these "prisons of the future"—resulted in a strongly worded opinion in which the federal court condemned certain of its features, suggesting that the prison, in the judge's words, inflicted "stark sterility and unremitting monotony" (*Madrid v. Gomez*, 1995, p. 1229) on prisoners and exposed them to overall conditions that "may press the outer bounds of what most humans can psychologically tolerate"(p. 1267) but left the basic regimen of segregation and isolation largely intact.

Here, too, the importance of context and situation has been ignored. Widespread prison management problems and gang-related infractions are best understood in systematic terms, as at least in large part the products of worsening overall institutional conditions. Viewing them instead as caused exclusively by "problem prisoners" who require nothing more than isolated and segregated confinement ignores the role of compelling situational forces that help to account for their behavior. It also overlooks the capacity of deteriorated prison conditions to continue to generate new replacements who will assume the roles of those prisoners who have been taken to segregation. Finally, the continued use of high levels of punitive isolation, despite evidence of significant psychological trauma and psychiatric risk (e.g., Grassian, 1983; Haney, 1997d; Haney & Lynch, 1997), reflects a legal failure to fully appreciate the costs of these potentially harmful social contexts—both in terms of immediate pain and emotional damage as well as their long-term effects on post-segregation and even post-release behavior.

The Retreat of the Supreme Court

The final component in the transformation of U.S. prison policy during this 25-year period came from the U.S. Supreme Court, as the Justices significantly narrowed their role in examining and correcting unconstitutionally cruel prison conditions as well as drastically redefining the legal standards that they applied in such cases. Ironically, the early constitutional review of conditions of confinement at the start of this historical period had begun on an encouraging note. Indeed, it was one of the things that helped fuel the early optimism about "evolving standards" to which we earlier referred. For example, in 1974, just three years after the SPE, the Supreme Court announced that "there is no iron curtain drawn between the Constitution and the prisons of this country" (*Wolff v. McDonnell,* 1974, pp. 556–567). Given the Warren Court's legacy of protecting powerless persons who confronted potent situations and adverse structural conditions, and the Court's legal realist tendencies to look carefully at the specific circumstances under which abuses occurred (e.g., Haney, 1991), hopes were raised in many quarters that a majority of the Justices would carefully evaluate the nation's worst prison environments, acknowledge their harmful psychological effects, and order badly needed reform.

However, a sharp right turn away from the possibility and promise of the Warren Court's view became evident at the start of the 1980s. The first time the Court fully evaluated the totality of conditions in a particular prison, it reached a very discouraging result. Justice Powell's majority opinion proclaimed that "the Constitution does not mandate comfortable prisons, and prisons . . . which house persons convicted of serious crimes cannot be free of discomfort" (*Rhodes v. Chapman,* 1981, p. 349). None of the Justices attempted to define the degree of acceptable discomfort that could be inflicted under the Constitution. However, Powell used several phrases that were actually taken from death penalty cases to provide a sense of just how painful imprisonment could become before beginning to qualify as "cruel and unusual": Punishment that stopped just short of involving "the *unnecessary* and *wanton* infliction of pain" (p. 345, citing *Gregg v. Georgia,* 1976, p. 173) would not be prohibited, pains of imprisonment that were not *"grossly* disproportionate to the severity of the crime" (p. 345, citing *Coker v. Georgia,* 1977, p. 592) would be allowed, and harm that was not *"totally* without penological justification" (p. 345, citing *Gregg v. Georgia,* p. 183) also would be acceptable (italics added).

The Supreme Court thus set a largely unsympathetic tone for Eighth Amendment prison cases and established a noninterventionist stance from which it has rarely ever wavered. Often turning a blind eye to the realities of prison life and the potentially debilitating psychological effects on persons housed in badly overcrowded, poorly run, and increasingly dangerous prisons, the Court developed several constitutional doctrines that both limited the liability of prison officials and further undermined the legal relevance of a careful situational analysis of imprisonment. For example, in one

---

"The Constitution does not mandate comfortable prisons, and prisons . . . which house persons convicted of serious crimes cannot be free of discomfort."—Former U.S. Supreme Court Justice Lewis F. Powell, Jr.

---

pivotal case, the Court decided that the notion that "overall prison conditions" somehow could produce a cruel and unusual living environment—a view that not only was psychologically straightforward but also had guided numerous lower court decisions in which overall conditions of confinement in particular prisons were found unconstitutional was simply "too amorphous" to abide any longer (*Wilson v. Seiter,* 1991, p. 304).

In the same case, the Court decisively shifted its Eighth Amendment inquiry from the conditions themselves to the thought processes of the officials responsible for creating and maintaining them. Justice Scalia wrote for the majority that Eighth Amendment claims concerning conduct that did not purport to be punishment required an inquiry into prison officials' state of mind—in this case, their "deliberate indifference" *(Wilson v. Seiter,* 1991). Justice Scalia also had rejected a distinction between short-term deprivations and "continuing" or "systemic" problems of the sort that might have made state of mind less relevant. The argument here had been that evidence of systemic problems would obviate the need to demonstrate state of mind on the part of officials who had presumably known about and tolerated them as part of the correctional status quo. Scalia said instead that although the long duration of a cruel condition might make it easier to establish knowledge and, hence, intent, it would not eliminate the intent requirement.

Prison litigators and legal commentators criticized the decision as having established a constitutional hurdle for conditions of confinement claims that was "virtually insurmountable" and speculated that the impossibly high threshold "reflects recent changes in public attitudes towards crime and allocation of scarce public resources" (Hall, 1993, p. 208). Finally, in 1994, the Court seemed to raise the hurdle to a literally insurmountable level by explicitly embracing the criminal law concept of "subjective recklessness" as the Eighth Amendment test for deliberate indifference *(Farmer v. Brennan,* 1994). In so doing, the Court shunned the federal government's concern that the new standard meant that that triers of fact would first have to find that "prison officials acted like criminals" before finding them liable *(Farmer v. Brennan,* 1994, p. 1980).

This series of most recent cases has prompted commentators to speculate that the Supreme Court is "headed toward a new hands-off doctrine in correctional law" (Robbins, 1993, p. 169) that would require lower courts "to defer to the internal actions and decisions of prison officials" (Hall, 1993, p. 223). Yet, the narrow logic of these opinions suggests that the Justices intend to keep not only their hands off the faltering prison system but their eyes averted from the realities of prison life as well. It is difficult to avoid the conclusion that the Court's refusal to examine the intricacies of day-to-day existence in those maximum security prisons whose deteriorated and potentially harmful conditions are placed at issue is designed to limit the liability of those who create and run them.

Unfortunately, the U.S. Supreme Court was not the only federal governmental agency contributing to this retreat from the meaningful analysis of conditions of confinement inside the nation's prisons and jails. In April 1996, the U.S. Congress passed legislation titled the Prison Litigation Reform Act (PLRA) that significantly limited the ability of the federal courts to monitor and remedy constitutional violations in detention facilities throughout the country. Among other things, it placed substantive and procedural limits on injunctions and consent decrees (where both parties reach binding agreements to fix existing problems in advance of trial) to improve prison conditions. The PLRA also impeded the appointment of "special masters" to oversee prison systems' compliance with court orders and appeared to forbid the filing of legal actions by prisoners for mental or emotional injury without a prior showing of physical injury. Although the full impact of this remarkable legislation cannot yet be measured, it seems to have been designed to prevent many of the problems that have befallen U.S. prisons from ever being effectively addressed. Combined with the Supreme Court's stance concerning prison conditions, the PLRA will likely contribute to the growing tendency to avoid any meaningful contextual analysis of the conditions under which many prisoners are now confined and also to a growing ignorance among the public about the questionable utility of prison as a solution to the nation's crime problem. . . .

Conclusion

When we conducted the SPE 25 years ago, we were, in a sense, on the cutting edge of new and developing situational and contextual models of behavior. Mischel's (1968) pathbreaking review of the inadequacy of conventional measures of personality traits to predict behavior was only a few years old, Ross and Nisbett (1991) were assistant professors who had not yet written about situational control as perhaps the most important leg in the tripod of social psychology, and no one had yet systematically applied the methods and theories of modem psychology to the task of understanding social contextual origins crime and the psychological pains of imprisonment. Intellectually, much has changed since then. However, without the renewed participation of psychologists in debates over how best to apply the lessons and insights of their discipline to the problems of crime and punishment, the benefits from these important intellectual advances will be self-limiting. It is hard to imagine a more pressing and important task for which psychologists have so much expertise but from which they have been so distanced and uninvolved than the creation of more effective and humane criminal justice policies.

Politicians and policymakers now seem to worship the very kind of institutional power whose adverse effects were so critically evaluated over the past 25 years.

Indeed, politicians and policymakers now seem to worship the very kind of institutional power whose adverse effects were so critically evaluated over the past 25 years. They have premised a vast and enormously expensive national policy of crime control on models of human nature that are significantly outmoded. In so doing, they have faced little intellectual challenge, debate, or input from those who should know better.

So, perhaps it is this one last thing that the SPE stood for that will serve the discipline best over the next 25 years. That is, the interrelated notions that psychology can be made relevant to the broad and pressing national problems of crime and justice, that the discipline can assist in stimulating badly needed social and legal change, and that scholars and practitioners can improve these policies with sound data and creative ideas. These notions are as germane now, and needed more, than they were in the days of the SPE. If they can be renewed, in the spirit of those more optimistic times, despite having lost many battles over the past 25 years, the profession still may help win the more important war. There has never been a more critical time at which to begin the intellectual struggle with those who would demean human nature by using prisons exclusively as agencies of social control that punish without attempting to rehabilitate, that isolate and oppress instead of educating and elevating, and that tear down minority communities rather than protecting and strengthening them.

References

American Friends Service Committee. (1971). *Struggle for justice: A report on crime and punishment.* New York: Hill & Wang.

Amnesty International. (1987). *Allegations of mistreatment in Marion Prison, Illinois, USA.* New York: Author.

Bandura, A. (1978). The self system in reciprocal determinism. *American Psychologist, 33,* 344–358.

Bandura, A. (1989). Mechanisms of moral disengagement. In W. Reich (Ed.), *Origins of terrorism: Psychologies, ideologies, theologies, states of mind* (pp. 161–191). New York: Cambridge University Press.

Bandura, A. (1991). Social cognitive theory of moral thought and action. In W. Kurtines & J. Gewirtz (Eds.), *Handbook of moral behavior and development: Vol. 1. Theory* (pp. 45–102). Hillsdale, NJ: Erlbaum.

Blumstein, A. (1993). Making rationality relevant—The American Society of Criminology 1992 Presidential Address. *Criminology, 31,* 1–16.

Brodt, S., & Zimbardo, P. (1981). Modifying shyness-related social behavior through symptom misattribution. *Journal of Personality and Social Psychology, 41,* 437–449.

Browning, C. (1993). *Ordinary men: Reserve Police Battalion 101 and the final solution in Poland.* New York: Harper Perennial.

Bureau of Justice Statistics. (1991). *Sourcebook of criminal justice statistics.* Washington, DC: U.S. Department of Justice.

Bureau of Justice Statistics. (1996). *Sourcebook of criminal justice statistics, 1996.* Washington, DC: U.S. Department of Justice.

Bureau of Justice Statistics. (1997a, May). *Correctional populations in the United States, 1995* (NCJ 163916). Rockville, MD: Author.

Bureau of Justice Statistics. (1997b, November). *Criminal victimization 1996: Changes 1995–96 with trends 1993–96* (Bureau of Justice Statistics Bulletin NCJ 165812). Rockville, MD: Author.

Bureau of Justice Statistics. (1998, January 18). *Nation's prisons and jails hold more than 1.7 million: Up almost 100,000 in a year* [Press release]. Washington, DC: U.S. Department of Justice.

Burks v. Walsh, 461 F. Supp. 934 (W.D. Missouri 1978).

Butterfield, F. (1995, April 12). New prisons cast shadow over higher education. *The New York Times*, p. A21.

Cahalan, M. W. (1986, December). *Historical corrections statistics in the United States, 1850–1984* (Bureau of Justice Statistics Bulletin NCJ 102529). Rockville, MD: Bureau of Justice Statistics.

Capps v. Atiyeh, 495 F. Supp. 802 (D. Ore. 1980).

Caprara, G., & Zimbardo, P. (1996). Aggregation and amplification of marginal deviations in the social construction of personality and maladjustment. *European Journal of Personality, 10*, 79–110.

Carr, S. (1995). Demystifying the Stanford Prison Study. *The British Psychological Society Social Psychology Section Newsletter 33*, 31–34.

Chambliss, W. (1994). Policing the ghetto underclass: The politics of law and law enforcement. *Social Problems, 41*, 177–194.

Christie, N. (1994). *Crime control as industry: Towards gulags, Western style?* (2nd ed.). London: Routledge.

Clements, C. (1979). Crowded prisons: A review of psychological and environmental effects. *Law and Human Behavior 3*, 217–225.

Clements, C. (1985). Towards an objective approach to offender classification. *Law & Psychology Review, 9*, 45–55.

Coker v. Georgia, 433 U.S. 584, 592 (1977).

Cullen, F. (1995). Assessing the penal harm movement. *Journal of Research in Crime and Delinquency, 32*, 338–358.

Dowker, F., & Good, P. (1992). From Alcatraz to Marion to Florence: Control unit prison in the United States. In W. Churchill & J. J. Vander Wall (Eds.), *Cages of steel: The politics of imprisonment in the United States* (pp. 131–151). Washington, DC: Maisonneuve Press.

Duke, M. (1987). The situational stream hypothesis: A unifying view of behavior with special emphasis on adaptive and mal-adaptive personality patterns. *Journal of Research in Personality, 21,* 239–263.

Dunbaugh, F. (1979). Racially disproportionate rates of incarceration in the United States. *Prison Law Monitor, 1,* 205–225.

Editorial: Inside the super-maximum prisons. (1991, November 24). *The Washington Post,* p. C6.

Ekehammar, B. (1974). Interactionism in personality from a historical perspective. *Psychological Bulletin, 81,* 1026–1048.

Farmer v. Brennan, 114 S. Ct. 1970 (1994).

Forer, L. (1994). A *rage to punish: The unintended consequences of mandatory sentencing.* New York: Norton.

Fowler, R. (1976). Sweeping reforms ordered in Alabama prisons. *APA Monitor, 7,* pp. 1, 15.

Freed, D. (1992). Federal sentencing in the wake of guidelines: Unacceptable limits on the discretion of sentences. *Yale Law Journal, 101,* 1681–1754.

Georgoudi, M., & Rosnow, R. (1985). Notes toward a contextualist understanding of social psychology. *Personality and Social Psychology Bulletin, 11,* 5–22.

Gibson, J. (1991). Training good people to inflict pain: State terror and social learning. *Journal of Humanistic Psychology, 31,* 72–87.

Grassian, S. (1983). Psychopathological effects of solitary confinement. *American Journal of Psychiatry, 140,* 1450–1454.

Gregg v. Georgia, 428 U.S. 153, 173 (1976) (joint opinion).

Gutterman, M. (1995). The contours of Eighth Amendment prison jurisprudence: Conditions of confinement. *Southern Methodist University Law Review, 48,* 373–407.

Hall, D. (1993). The Eighth Amendment, prison conditions, and social context. *Missouri Law Review, 58,* 207–236.

Haney, C. (1976). The play's the thing: Methodological notes on social simulations. In P. Golden (Ed.), *The research experience* (pp. 177–190). Itasca, IL: Peacock.

Haney, C. (1982). Psychological theory and criminal justice policy: Law and psychology in the "Formative Era." *Law and Human Behavior, 6,* 191–235.

Haney, C. (1983). The good, the bad, and the lawful: An essay on psychological injustice. In W. Laufer & J. Day (Eds.), *Personality theory, moral development, and criminal behavior* (pp. 107–117). Lexington, MA: Lexington Books.

Haney, C. (1991). The Fourteenth Amendment and symbolic legality: Let them eat due process. *Law and Human Behavior, 15,* 183–204.

Haney, C. (1993a). Infamous punishment: The psychological effects of isolation. *National Prison Project Journal, 8,* 3–21.

Haney, C. (1993b). Psychology and legal change: The impact of a decade. *Law and Human Behavior, 17,* 371–398.

Haney, C. (1994, March 3). Three strikes for Ronnie's kids, now Bill's. *Los Angeles Times,* p. B7.

Haney, C. (1995). The social context of capital murder: Social histories and the logic of mitigation. *Santa Clara Law Review, 35,* 547–609.

Haney, C. (1997a). Psychological secrecy and the death penalty: Observations on "the mere extinguishment of life." *Studies in Law, Politics, and Society, 16,* 3–68.

Haney, C. (1997b). Psychology and the limits to prison pain: Confronting the coming crisis in Eighth Amendment law. *Psychology, Public Policy, and Law, 3,* 499–588.

Haney, C. (1997c). Violence and the capital jury: Mechanisms of moral disengagement and the impulse to condemn to death. *Stanford Law Review, 46,* 1447–1486.

Haney, C. (1997d). *The worst of the worst: Psychological trauma and psychiatric symptoms in punitive segregation.* Unpublished manuscript, University of California, Santa Cruz.

Haney, C. (1998). *Limits to prison pain: Modem psychological theory and rational crime control policy.* Washington, DC: American Psychological Association.

Haney, C., Banks, W., & Zimbardo, P. (1973). Interpersonal dynamics in a simulated *prison. International Journal of Criminology and Penology, 1,* 69–97.

Haney, C., & Lynch, M. (1997). Regulating prisons of the future: A psychological analysis of supermax and solitary confinement. *New York Review of Law and Social Change, 23,* 101–195.

Haney, C., & Pettigrew, T. (1986). Civil rights and institutional law: The role of social psychology in judicial implementation. *Journal of Community Psychology, 14,* 267–277.

Haney, C., & Specter, D. (in press). Legal considerations in treating adult and juvenile offenders with special needs. In J. Ashford, B. Sales, & W. Reid (Eds.), *Treating adult and juvenile offenders with special needs.* Washington, DC: American Psychological Association.

Haney, C., & Zimbardo, P. (1977). The socialization into criminality: On becoming a prisoner and a guard. In J. Tapp & F. Levine (Eds.), *Law, justice, and the individual in society: Psychological and legal issues* (pp. 198–223). New York: Holt, Rinehart & Winston.

Hepburn, J. (1973). Violent behavior in interpersonal relationships. *Sociological Quarterly, 14,* 419–429.

Hilliard, T. (1976). The Black psychologist in action: A psychological evaluation of the Adjustment Center environment at San Quentin Prison. *Journal of Black Psychology, 2,* 75–82.

Human Rights Watch. (1997). *Cold storage: Super-maximum security confinement in Indiana.* New York: Author.

Immarigeon, R. (1992). The Marionization of American prisons. *National Prison Project Journal, 7*(4), 1–5.

Jackson, G. (1970). *Soledad brother: The prison letters of George Jackson.* New York: Coward-McCann.

Jordan, H. (1995, July 8). '96 budget favors prison over college; "3 strikes" to eat into education funds. *San Jose Mercury News,* p. IA.

King, A. (1993). The impact of incarceration on African-American families: Implications for practice. *Families in Society: The Journal of Contemporary Human Services, 74,* 145–153.

Madrid v. Gomez, 889 F. Supp. 1146 (N.D. Cal. 1995).

Maguire, K., & Pastore, A. (Eds.). (1997). *Sourcebook of criminal justice statistics 1996* (NCJ 165361). Washington, DC: U.S. Government Printing Office.

Masten, A., & Garmezy, N. (1985). Risk, vulnerability and protective factors in developmental psychopathology. In F. Lahey & A. Kazdin (Eds.), *Advances in clinical child psychology* (pp. 1–52). New York: Plenum.

Mauer, M. (1990). *More young Black males under correctional control in US than in college.* Washington, DC: The Sentencing Project.

Mauer, M. (1992). Americans behind bars: A comparison of international rates of incarceration. In W. Churchill & J. J. Vander Wall (Eds.), *Cages of steel: The politics of imprisonment in the United States* (pp. 22–37). Washington, DC: Maisonneuve Press.

Mauer, M. (1995). The international use of incarceration. *Prison Journal, 75,* 113–123.

Mauer, M. (1997, June). *Americans behind bars: U.S. and international use of incarceration, 1995.* Washington, DC: The Sentencing Project.

McConville, S. (1989). Prisons held captive. *Contemporary Psychology, 34,* 928–929.

McEwan, A., & Knowles, C. (1984). Delinquent personality types and the situational contexts of their crimes. *Personality & Individual Differences, 5,* 339–344.

Milgram, S. (1974). *Obedience to authority: An experimental view.* New York: Harper & Row.

Miller, G. (1980). Giving psychology away in the '80s. *Psychology Today, 13,* 38ff.

Mischel, W. (1968). *Personality and assessment.* New York: Wiley.

Mischel, W. (1979). On the interface of cognition and personality: Beyond the person-situation debate. *American Psychologist, 34,* 740–754.

Mitford, J. (1973). *Kind and usual punishment: The prison business.* New York: Knopf.

Monahan, J., & Klassen, D. (1982). Situational approaches to understanding and predicting individual violent behavior. In M. Wolfgang & G. Weiner (Eds.), *Criminal violence* (pp. 292–319). Beverly Hills, CA: Sage.

Mumola, C. J., & Beck, A. J. (1997, June). *Prisoners in 1996* (Bureau of Justice Statistics Bulletin NCJ 164619). Rockville, MD: Bureau of Justice Statistics.

National Advisory Commission on Criminal Justice Standards and Goals. (1973). *Task force report on corrections.* Washington, DC: U.S. Government Printing Office.

Newman, G. (1988). Punishment and social practice: On Hughes's *The Fatal Shore. Law and Social Inquiry, 13,* 337–357.

Olivero, M., & Roberts, J. (1990). The United States Federal Penitentiary at Marion, Illinois: Alcatraz revisited. *New England Journal of Criminal and Civil Confinement, 16,* 21–51.

Patterson, G., DeBaryshe, B., & Ramsey, E. (1989). A developmental perspective on antisocial behavior. *American Psychologist, 44,* 329–335.

Perkinson, R. (1994). Shackled justice: Florence Federal Penitentiary and the new politics of punishment. *Social Justice, 21,* 117–132.

Pugh v. Locke, 406 F. Supp. 318 (1976).

Rhodes v. Chapman, 452 U.S. 337 (1981).

Robbins, I. (1993). The prisoners' mail box and the evolution of federal inmate rights. *Federal Rules Decisions, 114,* 127–169.

Ross, L., & Nisbett, R. (1991). *The person and the situation: Perspectives of social psychology.* New York: McGraw-Hill.

Sampson, R., & Lauritsen, J. (1994). Violent victimization and offending: Individual-, situational-, and community-level risk factors. In A. Reiss, Jr. & J. Roth (Eds.), *Understanding and preventing violence: Vol. 3. Social influences* (pp. 1–114). Washington, DC: National Research Council, National Academy Press.

Sandin v. Conner, 115 S. Ct. 2293 (1995).

Scull, A. (1977). *Decarceration: Community treatment and the deviant: A radical view.* Englewood Cliffs, NJ: Prentice Hall.

Smith, C. (1993). Black Muslims and the development of prisoners' rights. *Journal of Black Studies, 24,* 131–143.

Spain v. Procunier, 408 F. Supp. 534 (1976), aff'd in part, rev'd in part, 600 F.2d 189 (9th Cir. 1979).

Toch, H. (1985). The catalytic situation in the violence equation. *Journal of Applied Social Psychology, 15,* 105–123.

Tonry, M. (1995). *Malign neglect: Race, crime, and punishment in America.* New York: Oxford University Press.

Trop v. Dulles, 356 U.S. 86 (1958).

Veroff, J. (1983). Contextual determinants of personality. *Personality and Social Psychology Bulletin, 9,* 331–343.

von Hirsch, A. (1976). *Doing justice: The choice of punishment.* New York: Hill & Wang.

Wenk, E., & Emrich, R. (1972). Assaultive youth: An exploratory study of the assaultive experience and assaultive potential of California Youth Authority wards. *Journal of Research in Crime & Delinquency, 9,* 171–196.

Wicker, T. (1975). *A time to die.* New York: New York Times Books.

Wilson v. Seiter, 501 U.S. 294 (1991).

Wolff v. McDonnell, 418 U.S. 554, 556–7 (1974).

Wright, K. (1991). The violent and victimized in the male prison. *Journal of Offender Rehabilitation, 16,* 1–25.

Yackle, L. (1989). *Reform and regret: The story of federal judicial involvement in the Alabama prison system.* New York: Oxford University Press.

Yee, M. (1973). *The melancholy history of Soledad Prison.* New York: Harper's Magazine Press.

Zimbardo, P. (1973). On the ethics of intervention in human psychological research: With special reference to the Stanford Prison Experiment. *Cognition, 2,* 243–256.

Zimbardo, P. (1975). On transforming experimental research into advocacy for social change. In M. Deutsch & H. Hornstein (Eds.), *Applying social psychology: Implications for research, practice, and training* (pp. 33–66). Hillsdale, NJ: Erlbaum.

Zimbardo, R G. (1977). *Shyness: What it is and what to do about it.* Reading, MA: Addison-Wesley.

Zimbardo, P. G. (1979a). The psychology of evil: On the perversion of human potential. In T. R. Sarbin (Ed.), *Challenges to the criminal justice system: The perspective of community psychology* (pp. 142–161). New York: Human Sciences Press.

Zimbardo, P. G. (1979b). Testimony of Dr. Philip Zimbardo to U.S. House of Representatives Committee on the Judiciary. In J. J. Bonsignore et al. (Eds.), *Before the law: An introduction to the legal process* (2nd ed., pp. 396–399). Boston: Houghton Mifflin.

Zimbardo, P. G. (1994). *Transforming California's prisons into expensive old age homes for felons: Enormous hidden costs and consequences for California's taxpayers.* San Francisco: Center on Juvenile and Criminal Justice.

Zimbardo, R. G., & Andersen, S. (1993). Understanding mind control: Exotic and mundane mental manipulations. In M. Langone (Ed.), *Recover from cults: Help for victims of psychological and spiritual abuse* (pp. 104–125). New York: Norton.

Zimbardo, P. G., Haney, C., Banks, C., & Jaffe, D. (1974). The psychology of imprisonment: Privation, power, and pathology. In Z. Rubin (Ed.), *Doing unto others: Explorations in social behavior* (pp. 61–73). Englewood Cliffs, NJ: Prentice Hall.

Zimbardo, P. G., Pilkonis, P. A., & Norwood, R. M. (1975, May). The social disease called shyness. *Psychology Today,* pp. 69–70, 72.

My Life As a Prison Teacher[3]

By Robert Ellis Gordon
Christian Science Monitor, March 12, 2001

In the spring of 1997, I taught my last creative writing class in the Washington State prisons. This particular class lasted for three weeks, and ran from 9 a.m. to 3 p.m. every day. It took place at the Washington Corrections Center in Shelton, about a two-hour drive from my home in Seattle. Rather than make the long daily commute, I spent the weeks at the Shelton Super 8, and drove home for the weekends.

WCC Shelton is a medium-security facility, and is reputed to be one of the "softer" joints in the system.

Still, WCC Shelton is a prison. And after spending eight years driving around the state and teaching classes at prison after prison, I had come to view prisons—whether "soft" or "hard"—as spiritual emergency wards; as repositories of society's poorest, most vilified outcasts; as repositories for men and women who live in settings that are notable for their exceptionally high levels of psychic pain, self-loathing, pent-up frustration, hate, gore, fear of rape, desire to rape, proximity to evil, proximity to grace, the ever-present threat of sudden violence, and—above all—despair.

Making Streets Safer

As you might expect, teaching in such settings exacted a high emotional toll on me. Nevertheless, no job I've held before or since has made me feel more useful. I felt that through the act of teaching in prisons, I was contributing to crime prevention. I felt this intuitively when I was alone with my students, and I felt it intellectually based on studies I'd read.

One study in particular comes to mind. It was conducted by the National Institute of Justice—the research arm of the federal Justice Department—during the mid-to-late 1980s. The study followed 105,000 state prisoners during the first few years after their release. Among its major findings were these:

- Sixty-six percent of the entire group were rearrested for a felony or a serious misdemeanor within three years of their release.

---

3. This article first appeared in *The Christian Science Monitor* on September 11, 2000, and is reproduced with permission. Copyright © 2000 *The Christian Science Monitor*. All rights reserved. Online at *csmonitor.com*.

- Of those who volunteered to get a high school diploma while in prison, that number dropped to 45 percent.

- Those who received a two-year college degree while in prison were rearrested at a rate of 27.5 percent.

- Those who received a four-year college degree while in prison were rearrested at a rate of 12.5 percent.

This is a dramatic set of statistics, and one that ought to be as meaningful to governors, state legislators, law-enforcement officials, and other policymakers as it is to educators and social workers. These numbers should carry a great deal of weight for anyone who professes a belief in crime prevention.

Education Programs Decimated

Unfortunately, this is not, apparently, the case. For there has been no clamor for more and better educational programming. On the contrary, the pendulum has swung the other way. In my home state of Washington, for example, as part of a new "no frills" approach to incarceration, the community-college system within our prisons—once a model for the nation—has, by legislative fiat, been dismantled. Even high school degrees are no longer offered to those convicts who want them.

Sadly, Washington State is not alone. Education programs have been or are being eliminated in state after state.

According to a study out of the University of Louisville, nine states have dropped their education programs entirely since 1994, and 70 percent of the remaining states have suffered draconian cutbacks in education.

There are two primary reasons for this trend. The first is the elimination of Pell Grants—federal scholarships—for state and federal prisoners. These grants were formerly used to pay for books, teachers, and educational facilities. The Omnibus Crime Bill of 1994 put an end to this funding.

The second reason for the decimation of education programs is a new "lock 'em up and throw away the key" sentiment that has swept across the land. Of course, in most cases the key is not really thrown away. Sooner or later most prisoners are released. Indeed, approximately half a million prisoners are released every year.

Lacking education, which is to say marketable skills, confidence, and an expanded sense of possibilities, it is inevitable that many of these released prisoners—including the ones who would've acquired an education if it had been offered—will return to what they know best: the life of crime. Thus, the polity's desire for vengeance is being fulfilled at the price of public safety.

Did the Holocaust Really Happen?

As noted, my residency at WCC Shelton lasted for three weeks. The Friday of the second week was a pleasant, cloudless, balmy day in April.

Around 3:30 in the afternoon, I was ambling—briefcase packed with student stories in hand—from the Education Building toward Main Control.

I'd checked out of the Super 8 that morning. So today, I wouldn't be returning to a motel. Instead, once I reached Main Control and exchanged my staff badge for my car keys, I'd get on I-5 and drive two hours north to my home in Seattle for the weekend.

Although I was fiercely devoted to my students, and planned to spend the weekend reading their stories, I was physically and emotionally exhausted. I was looking forward to two days away from the "spiritual emergency ward."

WCC Shelton is spread out like a ranch, and in good weather it's a pleasant walk to the front gate. I could smell the evergreen trees that grew thickly on the hillside just west of the prison. I could discern a slight sea tang from the nearby Hood Canal.

I turned left at the infirmary, and slowed down to admire the garden by which it was bordered. While I was appreciating the flowers, I noticed two young convicts digging a ditch about 20 yards away. Both were young and white.

They were probably getting paid about 15 cents an hour, and they were giving the state its money's worth. One of them would dig a shovelful of dirt now and then, but mostly they were standing around shooting the breeze, shirtless in the sun, and soaking up the rays.

I could hear snatches of their conversation, and soon became aware that the topic of discussion was me. "No, I know him," one guy was saying to the other. "I had him at Greenhill. Dude's OK."

Greenhill is the state's maximum security prison for older juvenile offenders. Evidently, my defender had "graduated" (as does 80 to 90 percent of Greenhill's population) to adult prison.

"Hey teacher!" he yelled. "How ya' doin'?"

"Fine," I said. "Just fine."

"Going home?" my former student asked.

"Just for the weekend. I'll be back."

I started to walk again.

"Hey teacher!" my former student yelled, this time with a hint of urgency in his voice.

I stopped walking and put my heavy briefcase down on the sidewalk. I turned to face the young man.

"Did the Holocaust really happen?"

Odious Lies Will Flourish

My lighthearted mood vanished instantly. I knew what this question meant. It meant that these two young and quite possibly gullible men were being recruited by members of some white supremacist gang.

And now, thanks to the state legislature's elimination of education programs, the white supremacist recruiters stood an excellent chance of success.

Just a few years before, 40 percent of WCC Shelton's inmates were enrolled as full-time students. And just a few years before, I would've used my authority to enroll these two kids in school. There, they would've been disabused of their wacky and dangerous "revisionist" theories.

But the school had been dismantled. And in the absence of education, ignorance could and would run rampant throughout the institution, unchecked by any pocket of resistance. Hatred, based on odious lies, would flourish.

Worse yet, this scene—this birth of two new neo-Nazis—wasn't taking place only at Shelton. As a result of sharp reductions in funding for prison education throughout the US, this scene was being replicated in prison after prison, state after state.

I took a good look at these two friendly and still malleable kids, who didn't have a clue that I was Jewish. They were probably on their way to becoming eager, head-shaven, indoctrinated, hate-spewing, no-longer-malleable fanatics.

They seemed well on their way, in fact. Barring some reversal that I could certainly not foresee, their political religion would quickly and insidiously invade every facet of their lives.

And there is nothing quite as dangerous as a generation of fanatics, or as wrong-headed as the prison policies that create them.

Maybe He's Lying

"So did it happen or not?" asked my former student.

"Yes," I said. "It happened."

"I heard that it didn't," he said.

"Trust me. It happened," I said.

"Six million Jews?"

"Plus Gypsies," I said. "Six million plus Gypsies and homosexuals."

"See?" said my former student as he turned to his friend.

"Maybe he's lying," said the friend.

My former student looked over at me. "No [expletive]?" he said.

"No [expletive]."

"Well, I heard it never happened," he said again.

I shrugged, picked up my briefcase, and made a beeline for Main Control.

Behind Bars, New Effort to Care for the Dying[4]

By Sheryl Gay Stolberg
New York Times, April 1, 2001

A thin shaft of yellow light streams through the grate over the window in Robert Newman's cell. Mr. Newman, inmate No. 286040 at the Louisiana State Penitentiary here, shifts uncomfortably in his bed, fighting nausea and fatigue. At 46, he is gaunt and dying. AIDS has gutted his immune system. Hepatitis C has wrecked his liver.

Prison is a tough place to die, yet Mr. Newman's plight is not as grim as it once might have been. Three years ago, Angola, as the prison is called, opened a hospice. Mr. Newman, who is serving a 50-year sentence for holding up a string of banks and Winn-Dixie supermarkets, is the 42nd patient.

He sleeps in a real hospital bed, a big step up from his old metal cot. His cell in the infirmary has an open-door policy, which means the guards let him meander outside, to a fenced-in yard, if he has the strength. One day not long ago, Mr. Newman wished aloud for Raisin Bran. The next day, some appeared in his cell.

And unlike prisoners here in the past, Mr. Newman will not die alone. His fellow inmates, trained in hospice care, watch over him.

The hospice at Angola is a new answer to a pressing question in prisons: what to do with dying inmates.

Longer mandatory sentences, tough law-and-order policies that keep criminals behind bars even when they are physically no longer a threat to others, and a quadrupling of the nation's prison population over two decades have led to more dying prisoners. At the same time, the inmate population is becoming more middle-aged, so wardens envision a future of caring for more of the infirm. Inmate deaths rose to 3,029 in 1999 from 727 in 1980, according to Justice Department figures.

One positive development is that AIDS deaths have declined significantly in recent years, because of new drugs, so the prison death rate has held relatively steady. "However, that doesn't change the fact that we have more prisoners than ever, they have longer sentences and their average age is increasing," said Herbert Rosefield,

---

4. Article by Sheryl Gay Stolberg from *New York Times* April 1, 2001. Copyright © *New York Times*. Reprinted with permission

former president of the American Correctional Health Services Association, a group of prison health professionals. "All you have to do is look at the math, and you know what's going to happen."

In response, some prison officials, including Angola's warden, Burl Cain, advocate compassionate release, or medical parole. But victims' rights advocates counter that violent criminals, even feeble ones, should remain behind bars.

"We don't want to hear all this baloney about how when they get old and sick we need to let them out," said Sandy Krasnoff, executive director of Victims and Citizens Against Crime, a statewide group.

Louisiana, for instance, has banned medical parole for murderers. Angola's hospice doctor, Robert Barnes, said he would not waste his

---

"We don't want to hear all this baloney about how when they get old and sick we need to let them out."—**Sandy Krasnoff, executive director of Victims and Citizens Against Crime**

---

time drawing up the paperwork for Mr. Newman, even though he is eligible.

Against this backdrop, prisons across the country are increasingly turning to hospices as a humane alternative. The first prison hospices opened in 1987, when AIDS was even more of a medical crisis. Today, 19 states, including New York, offer hospice care for inmates and 14 have programs in development, according to the Volunteers of America, a nonprofit social services agency that is writing standards for the care of inmates nearing death.

"What is happening is quite remarkable, against all odds," said Dr. Ira Byock, who directs a program, financed by the Robert Wood Johnson Foundation, to improve care of the dying. Dr. Byock visited the Oregon State Penitentiary hospice, which, like Angola, relies on inmate volunteers. "What has emerged," he said, "is a commitment to one another, a human community."

The same might be said of Angola.

"I've bathed people, I've wiped butts, I've asked men if it's time to put on a diaper," said James West, a 45-year-old armed robber who helps lead the hospice volunteer corps. "If God does keep books, I hope he keeps books on what I'm doing now."

Perhaps no prison has embraced the hospice concept as heartily as Angola. A former plantation named for the country that was home to its slaves, Angola sits on 18,000 acres in the oxbow of the Mississippi River, bordered on three sides by water and on the fourth by the overgrown Tunica Hills.

To visit the prison is to step back in time. Inmates here like to say that the initials L.S.P., for Louisiana State Penitentiary, stand for "last slave plantation." Early one recent morning, a crew of prisoners in blue jeans marched along a road carrying sling blades over their shoulders. Guards on horseback accompanied them to their assignment: cutting grass on a hillside, for 4 cents an hour.

Angola is home to 5,108 of Louisiana's most violent criminals, 91 of them on death row. The vast majority, 85 percent, will never get out, because they are serving life sentences without the possibility of parole, or more than 20 years, known as "practical life." One-third of Angola's inmates are older than 45, compared with 13 percent nationally.

A walk though the infirmary brings the demographics to life. It is the prison version of a nursing home

A walk though the infirmary brings the demographics to life. It is the prison version of a nursing home; two dozen beds on an open ward are flanked on each side by cells. One patient, an old toothless man, Eugene Scott, whom the other inmates call Shippy because his head is as big as a boat, is dribbling in his wheelchair; a stroke has stripped him of his ability to speak. Another, fighting emphysema, is hooked to an oxygen tank; still another, blind from glaucoma, rolls about in bed.

None of these men are yet receiving hospice care, because none are within six months of dying. But they clearly benefit from the presence of the inmate hospice volunteers, who are on hand to push wheelchairs that need pushing or wipe noses that need wiping. The volunteers, for their part, say the program has transformed their lives.

Michael Shulark, convicted of murder in a drug deal that went bad, is among them. A compact man with a rough, scarred face whose nickname is Arizona because he did prison time there, Mr. Shulark blinked back tears as he talked. "Instead of always wanting something," he said, "I'm giving something."

Encouraged by his success as a volunteer, Mr. Shulark made contact with his grown daughter. "I got my daughter back because of this program," he said. "She had never heard nothing good about me."

The idea for the hospice came from the warden, Mr. Cain, a big-bellied, silver-haired man with a passion for publicity. On a recent afternoon, Mr.Cain was leafing through the script of a new Billy Bob

Thornton movie he said would be filmed at Angola. He took a break to offer his philosophy of what makes a well-run prison: "good food, good medicine, good playing and good praying."

Mr. Cain, who came to Angola in 1995, said he began to think about prison deaths when he presided over his first execution. As a Christian, he said, it bothered him that he did not talk to the condemned man about the man's soul. In 1997, he came across a newspaper article about hospices, which have a strong spiritual component. He decided Angola needed one.

Mr. Cain gave the assignment to his assistant warden for treatment, R. Dwayne McFatter, and a no-nonsense nurse, Tanya Tillman. Together with a New Orleans hospice worker, Carol Evans, they drafted a plan. But although the hospice concept is simple—no one should die in pain, or alone—putting it into practice in a prison was not easy.

Dying people often need powerful painkillers. But drugs are more likely to be abused in prison than on the outside, and a big worry of Ms. Tillman's is that the medicines she dispenses will be stolen or sold.

At a recent conference on prison hospices in Atlanta, drug diversion was one of the most popular topics. A prison doctor from California said painkiller tablets were often washed out of his patients' socks.

Angola permits hospice patients to receive visits from prison friends, called the "inmate family." But inmates often have scores to settle, and so the securities staff runs an "enemies check" on each visitor to prevent fights from erupting on the infirmary ward. "Anytime you have a movement of inmates," Mr. McFatter said, "it's a problem."

And not all dying inmates are docile; another Angola hospice patient, Antoine Williams, is locked in his infirmary cell. Like Mr. Newman, Mr. Williams has AIDS, and the new drugs no longer work for him. But Mr. Williams is being punished for having sex with other prisoners. He talks to his visitors through the food slot in his steel door.

Ms. Tillman said: "I don't want to see that man die in that cell with the door locked. But he needs to be in there until he is debilitated."

For Mr. Newman, the program is a huge relief. "I believe you should go natural, when it's your time to go," he said, in a voice made gravelly by years of hard living. "But it sure is nice to know that somebody is caring about you when you die. It takes a lot of the pressure off."

Prison officials say the program has not cost any extra money, but it has had the unusual effect of creating new rituals around death at Angola. Mr. Cain, with his typical Louisiana flair, acquired a horse-drawn hearse, and has made funeral processions to the prison cemetery, a pauper's field of white wooden crosses marked with each inmate's name and number, a stately affair.

Next door to the infirmary, the inmates have built a chapel, with skylights and a sculpture donated by a Pennsylvania artist who heard about the hospice. At the carpentry shop, inmate craftsmen have begun making elaborate coffins, beautiful pine boxes lined with quilted mattress pads that the assistant warden, Mr. McFatter, buys at Wal-Mart.

Among the carpenters is Eugene Redwine, a slight, gray-haired 73-year-old who has been incarcerated at Angola for 28 years. Running his hand over one of the freshly made boxes, the smell of wood chips still in the air, Mr. Redwine offered a simple explanation for his work.

"One of these," he said, "is going to be for me someday."

II. A Tangle of Intentions: Imprisonment at Cross-Purposes

This barbed wire lines a prison facility fence.

Editor's Introduction

Debates over the proper function of the American prison system generally center around several recurring questions. For one, what types of behaviors should be punished, and to what degree? While most contend that violent criminals should be incarcerated, there is sharp disagreement about whether or not imprisonment in itself is a form of rehabilitation, or if violent criminals should be rehabilitated at all. Perhaps even more contentious is the question of how to treat nonviolent criminals, especially drug offenders, who have comprised an increasingly larger segment of the prison population since the 1970s.

Underlying these issues is the question of what incarceration is supposed to accomplish. The oft-stated—and somewhat contradictory—goals of incarceration include retribution against criminals, deterring crime, removing criminals from the general population, rehabilitating criminals to make them functioning members of society, and compensating the victims of crimes. Some argue that the reasons used to justify the prison system may be different from what actually drive it—political ambitions, profit motives, and simple force of habit. The articles in Section II examine some of the varying opinions about the proper goals of incarceration.

In "The Left's Prison Complex," Eli Lehrer objects to several criticisms commonly leveled against the American prison system. He argues that the large number of African-Americans in prisons is not due to any inherent inequalities in our justice system and that the growth of prisons is not caused by the lobbying of those who stand to profit financially or politically from them. Instead, Lehrer asserts, prison growth has been stimulated by increased crime rates, which have since decreased due to more stringent prison policies.

Carl M. Cannon offers a different perspective on prison growth in "America: All Locked Up." He challenges some of the statistics that have been used to justify the prison boom, including the claims that only one out of 100 violent crimes are punished, that convicted rapists serve an average of only 60 days in prison, and that released criminals commit between 187 and 287 crimes per year. Cannon asserts that these statistics are inaccurate and claims that they have nevertheless led to the passing of sentencing laws, such as mandatory minimums, three-strikes laws, and truth-in-sentencing laws, the latter of which require prisoners to serve 85 percent of their terms before they are considered for parole.

The influence of victims in determining prison policies is often overlooked, but victims' rights groups have campaigned to toughen punishments for criminals, such as eliminating some mandatory release rules and, in some cases, encouraging the death penalty. In "Victims Against Vengeance," however, Francie Latour points to several cases in which victims of violent crimes or their relatives have requested lighter sentences for their persecutors, stressing reconciliation instead.

The Left's Prison Complex[1]

BY ELI LEHRER
NATIONAL REVIEW, OCTOBER 9, 2000

The Left knows a growth industry when it sees one. Ever since prominent left-wing journalist Mike Davis popularized the term "prison industrial complex" in a 1995 *Nation* article, self styled progressives have relentlessly derided America's burgeoning prison system as a racist, profit-driven monster that enriches corporations and wastes tax dollars while doing little to reduce crime.

The Left's attack on the prison system is wrong in every major respect. America's prison system doesn't discriminate against blacks, is not growing because of a search for profits, and has made America much safer than other countries. For the Left, attacking the prison system is little more than an excuse to recycle tired anti-capitalist canards.

Little evidence exists that black criminals face discrimination in the criminal-justice system. Black "overrepresentation" in that system is in the number of criminals arrested. Racist cops aren't responsible for this disparity: Blacks get arrested at the same high rates in cities like Atlanta and Washington where the political establishment is almost entirely African-American and the police forces reflect the population's ethnic makeup. In a study on sentencing disparity commissioned by the Center for Equal Opportunity, former University of Maryland professor Robert Lerner finds that arrested blacks get sent to prison at a lower rate than arrested whites in just about every category that the government measures. Lemer found that blacks were twice as likely to get off on rape charges, around 50 percent more likely to escape punishment when charged with simple assault, and a third more likely to beat the rap on drug dealing. The difference in favor of black offenders existed in 12 out of 14 categories of crime. (The exceptions were traffic felonies and a small category of miscellaneous offenses.)

Black murderers face shorter sentences than their white counterparts and (contrary to leftist dogma) make fewer trips to death row. Even when it comes to the federal law punishing crack possession much more harshly than powder cocaine possession—a favorite topic of Jesse Jackson and Al Sharpton—racism doesn't enter the picture. In his 1997 book *Race, Crime and the Law*, Harvard Law

School professor Randall Kennedy shows that the law passed with the enthusiastic support of black congressmen who saw crack becoming the drug of choice in their districts. The use of methamphetamine and heroin—predominantly by whites—has soared in the 1990s, while the penalties for this use have remained stable. Would black Americans be better off if the situation were reversed, and crack dealing went on uninterrupted in American inner cities while police cracked down on rural whites using methamphetamine? If this happened, civil rights leaders would organize protest marches in favor of stronger drug-enforcement efforts in inner cities—and would be right to do so.

Would black Americans be better off if . . . crack dealing went on uninterrupted in American inner cities while police cracked down on rural whites using methamphetamine?

It's Not About the Money

The contention that the quest for profits has driven America's fourfold increase in prison capacity since 1980 is equally specious. Private-prison operators, a chief bugbear of the Left, incarcerate a measly 5 percent of America's convicts. Prisons contract out more services than they did 15 years ago, but so do nearly all other government agencies. The overwhelming majority of prison services remain in the hands of money-losing government bureaucracies. Unlike their military-industrial counterparts, which produce some of America's leading exports and sell civilian goods ranging from jetliners to computer hardware, major prison-related producers sell little outside of America's borders and almost nothing to private citizens. While a few states, California and Tennessee most prominently, do count corrections-industry groups among their most powerful lobbies, they remain exceptions. No sizeable cities have prison-reliant economies, and few people outside of declining farm towns actually want to live near prisons. Indeed, the presence of a large jail proved a major stumbling block in the effort to revitalize Chicago's South Loop.

It's not profits, but well-founded public outrage over criminals being set loose too soon that has driven America's gradual increase in length of prison sentences. In the early 1970s, as crime increased and prison sentences decreased, annual Gallup polls showed huge increases in Americans' fear of crime. The number of Americans telling pollsters that crime was a major political issue likewise increased sharply, as did public support for stiffer sentences.

Public sentiment was right. British researcher Donald E. Lewis's comprehensive examination of studies on the correlation between sentence length and crime rates (published in the *British Journal of Criminology*) concludes that doubling the length of the sentence for a crime will cut the likelihood that crime will be committed by a little less than half. In a 1994 report on national sentencing policies published by the National Institute of Justice, Michael K. Block—a former member of the federal sentencing commission—found that violent criminals, on average, spent a little over three months in prison per reported crime, and even murderers were turned loose

---

Mapped against each other, America's rates of incarceration and overall crime form a neat X: As incarceration rates rose, crime fell.

---

after serving an average of about five years. Sentences have increased a bit since 1994, but remain shockingly low. "There are too many criminals committing too many crimes," wrote Block. "We find ourselves [building more prisons] because for most of the last half of the 20th century, sentencing practices have not been harsh enough."

Locking up criminals for longer periods of time has proven one of America's most effective anticrime strategies. Honest liberals can't dispute James Q. Wilson's observation that "coincident with rising prison population there began in 1979–80 a steep reduction in the crime rate as reported by the victimization surveys." American property-crime rates peaked in 1974, fell slightly through most of the rest of the decade and then began a steep decline in the early 1980s. Violent-crime rates followed the same trendline, but rose for a few years in the late 1980s as crack swept inner cities, before dropping sharply in the 1990s. In 1973, nearly 60 percent of American households fell victim to property crimes. In 1999, fewer than 20 percent did. The same holds for violent crime: Had the 1999 crime rates been the same as those of 1990, America would have seen about 7,800 additional murders, 20,000 or so additional rapes, and nearly a quarter-million more armed attacks. Mapped against each other, America's rates of incarceration and overall crime form a neat X: As incarceration rates rose, crime fell.

Despite these facts, a widely cited 1997 report from the Sentencing Project, a left-leaning advocacy group, argued that America's high imprisonment rate has not reduced crime—because nations with lower incarceration rates are safer than the U.S. The study conveniently begins its analysis right before cheap, violence-inducing crack became widely available in America's cities, and ends it just as the epidemic began to wane. The crack epidemic drove up crime rates in the early years of the study, while the effects of improved policing and greater imprisonment didn't really take hold until after the period studied. Adding data from 1997, 1998, and 1999—years that saw some of the largest reductions in crime since the government started systematically tracking crime statistics in the 1920s—would have made the study's data into an argument for more incarceration.

The bulk of the evidence shows that longer sentences really do work. And an honest look at the international data presents a good case for building prisons: A 1998 study from the British Home Office, their equivalent of the Justice Department, cited the U.S. as one of only two major Western countries to see their crime rates drop between the late 1980s and late 1990s. Canada, France, England, and Switzerland all have more crime per capita than the United States. A study commissioned by the Justice Department's Bureau of Justice Statistics found that in 1998, Englishmen were twice as likely as Americans to have their cars stolen, about a third more likely to get mugged by an armed assailant, and nearly ten times more likely to have their home broken into while it was occupied. The study's authors suggest an explanation: "An offender's risk of being caught, convicted and incarcerated has been rising in the United States but falling in England."

Indeed, many of the other factors that social scientists believe may reduce crime in America are present in other countries that put fewer people in prison and have seen crime fall far more slowly. Canada and Britain have both seen comparable economic prosperity during the late 1990s. Canada's police departments have made the same switch toward community policing as America's, which was itself based on British methods. While a shrinking population of men between their mid teens and late twenties did help reduce America's crime rates, the nation's youth population has begun rising again—even as nearly all other industrialized countries have seen much greater drops in their youth populations, and small or nonexistent drops in crime. Indeed, high-poverty American cities like Garden Grove, Calif., and McAllen, Tex.—not coincidentally located in states that have invested heavily in prison infrastructure—have seen their crime rates drop sharply even though their high-schoolaged populations have skyrocketed.

An Attack on Capitalism

America's prison system isn't perfect. "There's no intrinsic reason why conservatives should support [prisons]. They are big, they cost a lot of money, and they expand the role of the state," says Pat Nolan of the Justice Fellowship, the publicpolicy arm of Charles Colson's Prison Fellowship. "Take the DMV, string barbed wire, and give the clerks guns and you'll get the idea." Violence and brutality fill America's prisons: Between a quarter and a third of male prisoners get raped by their fellow inmates. Black—and white—nationalist gangs control many prisons and all too often have free rein to recruit new members.

For the Left, solving these problems is often beside the point; most leftists simply want to attack capitalism. "The companies that actually imprison people are only a small part of what's going on. We're talking about architects, foodservice providers, companies that make software, the prison guards' unions," says Colorado journalist Joel Dyer, author of *The Perpetual Prisoner Machine: How America Profits from Crime*. "The real problem is the structure of our economy." Rising incarceration rates also provide an excuse for the Left to talk about many of its favorite issues. "You can use [America's imprisonment rate] to talk about class; you can deal with globalization and racism and poverty," says Daniel Burton-Rose of the Prison Activist Resource Center. "It lets you take on the entire system and educate people about why capitalism doesn't work." The situation in academia is little better. As the University of Delaware's Kenneth Haas, coeditor of the widely used anthology *The Dilemmas of Corrections*, correctly points out: "They've been writing articles for 20 years about the thesis that unemployment rates and imprisonment rates are linked. What you get is a lot of work done by quantitative sociologists who have an enormous leftward bias. They say nice things about each other to the National Science Foundation . . . and nothing changes."

The Left's attack on the prison system has little to do with its nominal target and a lot to do with loathing for capitalism. America's prison system could stand some improvement, but we should remember that people go to prison because they commit crimes, not because others want to make money.

America: All Locked Up[2]

BY CARL M. CANNON
NATIONAL JOURNAL, AUGUST 15, 1998

In what has become a familiar ritual in federal courthouses, U.S. District Court Judge Joseph Goodwin peered at the young, small-time marijuana grower—the kind who once would have qualified for an alternative-sentencing program—and gave him five years in prison.

"This sentence seems unduly harsh," Goodwin told the defendant, 23-year-old Bobby Lee Sothen of Cabell County, W.Va. But there was not much Goodwin could do. In the mid-1980s, Congress took the responsibility for weighing the circumstances of drug cases out of the judiciary's hands. In federal courts nowadays, every sentence is the same if the amount of drugs involved is the same. If there is any discretion to be exercised, it belongs to prosecutors in deciding how defendants are charged. The U.S. Attorney's office in Huntington, W.Va., cut Bobby Lee Sothen no slack. He got, the "mandatory minimum" sentence of 60 months.

That was in May. In June, a jury in Denton, Texas, deliberated all of 48 minutes before sentencing Eddie DeWayne Perot, a 34-year-old man with a full-time job, a fiancée and a new baby, to two life terms in prison for two cases of drunk driving. The convictions were his third and fourth for driving under the influence, which made them felonies. And because Perot had previously been convicted of two minor theft charges, prosecutors charged him under Texas' habitual offender statute—even though Perot had not injured anyone. He hadn't, in fact, even been in a car accident. But the prosecutor is running for a local judgeship, and, well, that's the way it goes in Texas these days.

"We incarcerate 'em by the truckload," says Ernest Tosh, Perot's lawyer. "We're known for the death penalty, but not only do we kill 'em, we also like to stack 'em deep."

In July, 19-year-old Andre Terial Wilks of North Hills, Calif., received a sentence of 25 years to life under California's "Three strikes and you're out" law. His crime? Breaking a car window and stealing a cell phone. Wilks, who had two purse-snatching convic-

---

tions on his record from when he was 16, had turned down a plea bargain, believing seven years in prison was too much time for a cell phone.

To Wilks' mother, Pamela Jones, her son's refusal to cop a plea revealed his immaturity, not his lack of contrition. It also showcased the capriciousness of the criminal justice system. "There are people doing attempted murders who don't get that much time," Jones complained bitterly. In an interview in early August, Eddie Perot's mom said the same thing. "I'm 61 years old, so I'll never see my son on the outside again," she said. "You've no idea how rough that is."

"An Orgy of Incarceration"

It is tempting to view such cases as aberrations, but they are more common than policy-makers might imagine. As hundreds of thousands of families have discovered in recent years, the United States, in the name of controlling crime, has embarked on a vast social experiment. It is an experiment with no name, only a theory, a huge price tag and droves, of statistics.

The theory is that a substantial amount of the nation's street crime is committed by a small number of bad actors, And that putting them behind bars for exceedingly long stretches of time— maybe their whole lives—will make all of us safer. The statistics come in any form you like, from the falling national murder rate to the exorbitant estimates of how many crimes the average felon would have committed had he been out on the street.

The problem with the theory is that it may apply to only a small portion of those being incarcerated. Indeed, many of the statistics upon which the theory is based are myths. But with politicians and the public clamoring for safer streets, there appears to be no turning back. The upshot is that with few dissenting voices and, paradoxically, at a time of sustained economic prosperity that makes America the envy of the world, the authorities are incarcerating people at a rate approaching five times the historical norm.

If local jails are included, the United States will usher in the new century with something close to 2 million of its residents behind bars, twice as many as just 10 years ago. On any given day, one in three black men in several large American cities, including Washington, D.C., is either incarcerated or on probation or parole. Women inmates are the fastest-growing subpopulation in prison, and estimates of the number of minor children with one or both parents behind bars are as high as 1.5 million.

"It's an orgy of incarceration," says Marc Mauer, assistant director of the Sentencing Project, a liberal group that favors alternatives to lengthy prison terms. "It represents a societal commitment to imprisonment on a scale that would have been unthinkable a quarter of a century ago in this, or any other, country. Now, it's business as usual."

The government began compiling credible data on the number of people in prison in 1925. That year, 79 out of every 100,000 Americans served time in state or federal prisons. At the end of the Roaring 1920s, the incarceration index had gone up slightly—to over 100. For 50 years, that is where it stayed, with only a few blips. The high point, 137 out of 100,000, came in 1939. A low period came in the late 1960s, when it dipped below 100 and stayed there for seven consecutive years, culminating in a low of 93 in 1972.

Then something happened.

In 1973, the incarceration number inched upward. It went up again in 1974 and in 1975. In fact, it kept climbing every year for the rest of the decade. By 1980, the percentage of Americans behind bars surpassed the record year of 1939. But it never went back down. It went up again every year in the 1980s as well. By 1985, the number topped 200—twice the historical norm. By 1995, the rate of Americans behind bars doubled again—to 411. At the beginning of August, Justice Department figures for 1997 showed yet another increase—to 445. If local jails are included, more than 1.7 million adults are currently incarcerated.

To accommodate all these inmates, the nation has embarked on a prison building binge. Between 1990 and 1995, 168 state and 45 federal prisons were constructed. Rural counties covet them the way they once did Japanese auto plants. Private-sector prisons are all the rage. The largest private firm, the Corrections Corp. of America, runs 78 prisons in 25 states.

Behind the staggering increase in the incarceration rate are changes in the criminal statutes in Washington and the state capitals. These laws are not on the verge of being repealed, and in some cases, are only beginning to be felt. They include mandatory minimums for drug offenses; federal and state three-strikes statutes; and "truth-in-sentencing" laws, which require criminals to serve 85 percent of their terms before being eligible for parole.

"We've gone on this prison-building rampage," says Morgan Reynolds, a Texas A&M economics professor who is also director of the criminal justice department at the National Center for Policy Analysis, a Dallas-based conservative think tank, "But we've made an incontrovertible increase in public safety because of it."

Is Reynolds correct? Certainly most politicians think so. Or to be more precise, after decades of concern for the welfare of defendants, liberals have essentially thrown in the towel and have become indistinguishable from conservatives on the issue. "Stack 'em deep" has become national policy, and in the rush to incarcerate, profound questions have been getting short shrift:

- Is the increase in the prison population really a key reason that crime has been declining nationally for the past four years, or are there other, more salient, factors?

- What are the hidden social costs of the current policy, above and beyond the money it takes to warehouse upwards of 1.5 million people?

- In trolling for culprits with such a fine net, is the criminal justice system catching people who are not dangerous and for whom lengthy prison terms are a waste, if not an injustice?

"Let 'em Rot"

Violence has always been a defining trait of the American experience. So have the efforts of elected officials to control it. Discussions of deterrents invariably turn into discussions of the root causes of crime. Liberals tend to stress such factors as poverty, the cycle of domestic violence and a lack of gun control. Conservatives focus on such issues as violent Hollywood fare, the removal of school prayer and the degradation of family, values. But in recent years, voters have sent an unmistakable message that they don't really care about what causes crime, they just want something done to make them safer in their homes and on their streets.

The prevailing public mood toward criminals was summed up in the headline over a 1994 essay written for *The Wall Street Journal* by Princeton University proffessor John J. Dilulio Jr. that said simply: "Let 'em rot." In the late 1980s and early 1990s, Dilulio was in the vanguard of a group of conservative scholars who challenged the nation's courts, parole boards and lawmakers to get tougher on convicted criminals. From 1960–80, they pointed out, the number of violent crimes in the United States almost quintupled, going from 288,000 to more than 1.3 million. Property crimes increased from some 3 million to 12 million. At the same time, the number of people in prison increased only from 213,000 to 316,000. Law-abiding Americans were far less safe in 1980 than in 1960, while criminals incurred only a marginally greater risk of going to prison.

"People got tired of that," former Attorney General Edwin Meese III says succinctly. Meese and other conservatives, determined to turn things around, began focusing on policing techniques and sentencing procedures, paying special attention to repeat offenders.

In time, catchphrases and statistics from their work became a kind of litany recited by politicians, especially conservatives, every time a crime bill was up for consideration: Only one out of 100 violent crimes results in a prison sentence. A rapist gets an average sentence of 60 days. Only 6 percent of the criminals commit 70 percent of the crimes. Juvenile crime is getting worse, with a generation of "superpredators" on the horizon. Prison does not rehabilitate. The average criminal commits between 187 and 287 crimes a year while out on the street. And those crimes cost society far more money than incarceration. In other words, prison pays for itself and makes society safer in the process. Locking more people up is not only the right thing to do, it is a good deal.

The lessons implicit in this mantra were obvious: The "medical model" of the 1960s and 1970s, which treated criminality almost as a disease and incarceration as a last resort, was utterly flawed. The solution was judges, who would mete out longer prison sentences.

By the late 1980s, this view became a national consensus, and politicians who understood it fared better than those who did not. California Gov. George Deukmejian quipped in his 1986 campaign that when he promised criminals a "California cooler," he wasn't talking about a beverage. George Bush vowed to double spending on federal prisons when he campaigned for president, and criticized Massachusetts Gov. Michael S. Dukakis because a convicted killer named William Horton, while on furlough from a Massachusetts prison, raped a woman and stabbed her boyfriend. In 1992, then-Arkansas-Gov. Bill Clinton vowed to fund 100,000 more law enforcement officers. "We need to put more police on the street and more criminals behind bars," he said.

Funny Numbers

But here's a question often lost in the shuffle: Is the lore undergirding these get-tough policies even true?

- Sen. Phil Gramm, R-Texas, popularized the notion that a rapist can "expect" to serve 60 days behind bars. Gramm also said the average term for murder is 1.8 years in prison. These figures come from Morgan Reynolds, the Texas A&M economist, who arrived at them by dividing the average time served by rapists into the total number of rapes committed. Thus, those who never got arrested or convicted bring down the average. The real figures for homicide, including involuntary manslaughter, is more than 10 years, according to the U.S. Bureau of Justice Statistics. The Justice Department also says that seven years—not 60 days—is the average term for a convicted rapist.

- The statistic that only one out of 100 violent crimes is ever punished is a favorite of the conservative Council on Crime in America. It is also fanciful. The council took the number of violent crimes in a recent year—10 million—and divided it by the number of people sentenced to prison for crimes of violence—100,000. But a considerable number of the 100,000 are sentenced for more than one violent act. Second, half of the crimes in this category—simple assaults without injury—are not felonies at all and thus not punishable by prison terms. The council did not count those sentenced to jail, the common disposition in misdemeanor assaults, or to juvenile institutions. Third, the 10 million figure is derived from victimization surveys. Most of them are not even reported to the police. Finally, even in cases of serious violence, the main reason the perpetrator wouldn't go to prison is that he was never caught.

- The claim that the typical repeat offender commits between 187 and 287 crimes per year when on the street was made in the late 1970s by the Rand Corp. It was based on interviews with 2,190 inmates in California, Texas and Michigan. This study had problems, not the least of which was that it assumed that thieves admitting to burglaries at a rate of one every other day could go a whole year and not get caught. In 1994, Rand itself essentially disavowed the estimate in an extraordinary two-page document that received little or no coverage in the press. The fact sheet explains that in the 1970s study, 10 percent of the inmates were extremely active, committing more than 600 crimes apiece. The typical inmate—the median in the sample—reported committing 15 crimes a year. The fact sheet ends by citing the work of two University of California (Berkeley) researchers, Franklin E.

- Zimring and Gordon Hawkins, who estimate that California's recent prison buildup has prevented between three and four felonies per inmate per year—"primarily property offenses."

The most thorough study of recidivism, done in 1986 by the National Research Council, produced the estimate that "active violent offenders" probably commit two to four violent crimes a year, while "active nonviolent offenders" were responsible for five to 10 property crimes a year.

Nonetheless, the original Rand figure lives on and on. In 1988, a Justice Department economist named Edwin Zedlewski took the estimate of 187–287 annual crimes, assigned dollar costs to each of those crimes and concluded that the $8.6 billion spent on the nation's prisons and jails was a bargain. In Zedlewski's extrapolations, the cost to society of 187 crimes was $430,000 a year—ten times the cost of incarceration. In 1989, Justice Department official Richard B. Abell used these figures to argue that "two good ideas" (fiscal conservatism and getting tough with criminals) were not really at odds. Amplifying Zedlewski's estimates, Abell contended that for every 100 offenders put behind bars, society could save about $40 million in costs associated with crime.

Noting that by 1989 the United States had recently incarcerated an additional half-million felons, Zimring and Hawkins responded caustically that if the original Rand study had been accurate, American would be crime-free.

The claim that crime may be down but "the demographic fuses of America's ticking crime bomb are already burning" was John Dilulio's evocative warning that a generation of juvenile "super-predators" was just over the horizon. The next wave, Dilulio warned in a 1995 *Weekly Standard* article were younger, meaner and more likely to use guns than their predecessors. Elected officials seized on this dire scenario. Former Sen. Robert Dole featured "superpreda-tors" in his 1996 presidential campaign. Rep. Bill McCollum, R-Fla., originally named his get-tough juvenile crime bill the Violent Juve-nile Predator Act of 1996. A version of that bill is still pending in Congress, and Clinton has made several pitches in favor of it. There's just one nagging little problem, however. Juvenile crime has been plummeting almost since the moment Dilulio spoke.

"There's no proof whatsoever of a coming plague of superpreda-tors. It's nonsense," scoffs Jerome G. Miller, president of the National Center on Institutions and Alternatives, a liberal group in Alexandria, Va. "Dilulio misuses statistics terribly."

To his credit, Dilulio has displayed some grace under fire, and an open mind as well. Last year, he conceded that "most kids"—notice he did not say superpredators—who get in serious trouble with the law need adult guidance. "And they won't find suitable role models in prison," he added. Earlier this year, he confessed to being puzzled by the drop in juvenile crime, adding, "This is a humbling time for all crime analysts. "He has also broken with conservatives by oppos-ing, mandatory minimums for first-time drug offenders.

Fodder for Attack Ads

Historically, this, is the way the endless debates about criminal justice work. Theories come in and out of vogue. If an approach proves to be based on faulty premises, well, laws can be changed. That once happened, in fact, with mandatory minimums in drug cases, which were passed in 1950 and repealed in 1970 when the federal prisons were filling up with minor drug offenders. That year, no less a law-and-order man than George Bush, then a congressman representing Houston, Texas, stood in the well of the House and noted that federal judges were a most unanimously opposed to the minimums. "Practicality requires a sentence structure which is generally acceptable to the courts, to prosecutors and to the general public," Bush said.

But in the current contentious political climate, the political system seems locked in place. "The reason is, the most inexperienced political campaign consultant can write a 30-second ad that says, 'Congressman Smith voted to let hundreds of crack dealers out of federal prison,'" says Eric E. Sterling, president of the Criminal Justice Policy Foundation, which is seeking to overturn mandatory minimums. "That can be the end of a campaign."

It happened barely three weeks ago in Georgia. Gubernatorial candidate Roy Barnes, a Democrat, found himself on the receiving end of just such an attack ad from Republican candidate Guy Millner over the issue of crime. Millner's campaign unearthed a 1981 state Senate vote in which Barnes supported a measure designed to streamline parole procedures. The ad does not point out that the measure was in response to a federal court order to reduce prison overcrowding, that it involved only first-time offenders—or that it passed the state Senate 48–0. It just says, "Roy Barnes *is* soft on crime. And he's too liberal for Georgia."

Such casual demagoguing about crime helps explain why in 1995, after the U.S. Sentencing Commission recommended that crack cocaine and powder cocaine be treated the same under the law, Congress refused to act—despite overwhelming evidence that the impact of the differential has been borne almost exclusively by black defendants. (The 1986 crime bill, voted into law, called for treating crimes involving crack as 100 times more serious than those involving powder cocaine.)

In response to similar complaints about three-strikes laws, law-and-order advocates insist that they have made our streets safe. Earlier this summer, while announcing that California's crime rate plunged to a 30-year low, California Attorney General Dan Lungren, a Republican candidate for governor, estimated that the steady, four-year decline in rime has resulted in 800,000 fewer crimes, including 6,000 rapes and 4,000 murders—and gave credit to three-strikes.

Surely, Lungren is overselling the deterrent effects of three-strikes. But just as surely, increased incarceration must have some impact on lowering the nation's crime rates, as even many liberal academics concede. But how much? Criminologists from across the ideological spectrum often cite two other factors that may have more to do with the downward trend of crime in America. The first is the favorable demographic trend in the country. Overall, the population is getting older. Call it the geezer factor, but as the proportion of older Americans has increased and the baby boomers have moved into middle age, the segment of 15- to 29-year-olds—the prime years of criminality—has shrunk from 23 percent in 1990 to 21 percent today.

A second, and perhaps more important, factor is the revolution in policing techniques. Clinton often refers to improved policing by the shorthand expression "community policing," which evokes neighborhood-watch programs, uniformed cops playing midnight basketball, officers patrolling parks on bicycles and various other outreach programs designed, to make officers a welcome presence in the community. In truth, the greatest success stories in policing during the 1990s have come in cities using nearly the opposite technique, known in law enforcement as "proactive" policing. Proactive policing entails rousting a lot of suspicious-looking characters, holding watch commanders responsible for their precincts and vigorously arresting and prosecuting every crime, no matter how small.

What the two approaches have in common is that they get cops out of patrol cars and station houses and into the community. Both have met with success. Los Angeles, which pioneered proactive policing, has, in the wake of the 1991 Rodney King case, embraced a community approach. So have St. Louis and Denver. New York and Houston, to cite the two most successful examples, have embraced an aggressive proactive policing strategy.

"You have had major increases in incarceration and clearly that helps," says Meese. "But I believe the changes in policing are the most important factor in lowering the crime rate."

If so, then Bill Clinton deserves some of the credit because, whatever he wants to call it, he is responsible for helping the communities of this country get another 100,000 officers out on the street as part of the Community-Oriented Policing Services program he insisted on in the 1994 crime bill.

By that year, Congress was in a well-established pattern of passing a crime bill every two years—every election year. This trend began in 1986, with a tragedy that everyone who was in Washington at the time remembers well, the death of Maryland basketball star Len Bias.

From Len Bias to Polly Klass

In June 1986, Bias was drafted by the Boston Celtics and was poised to make millions of dollars to play with Larry Bird and other legends in Boston Garden. The next day, he was dead of a cocaine overdose. That summer, crack cocaine and its associated violence and health risks exploded on the public consciousness. New York City reported a sharp increase in murder, robbery and assault in neighborhoods where crack had taken hold. On June 27, a week after Len Bias was buried, cocaine killed Don Rogers, a defensive back for the Cleveland Browns. Over the July 4 recess, all Democratic House Speaker Thomas P. "Tip" O'Neill Jr. and Majority Leader Jim Wright heard back home was drugs, guns and cocaine.

"The chemistry to create an issue was there—and Bias lit it," former Rep. Tony Coelho, D-Calif., later recalled.

Back in Washington, O'Neill convened a July 23 meeting with the chairmen of 11 House committees. He told them to fashion a sweeping bipartisan bill aimed at drug control and to bring it to the floor for a vote by September. The $1.7 billion plan passed the House 392-16 and the Senate by a voice vote. The media coverage scarcely mentioned the feature that would be the law's enduring and controversial legacy: the "mandatory minimums" that would fill the federal prisons with small-time dealers, especially those who dealt crack. A crack dealer caught with 5 grams—a handful of "rocks" worth roughly $500—automatically gets five years in federal prison, the same as someone selling 500 grams of powder cocaine.

When Clinton was first elected president, groups such as the Families Against Mandatory Minimums Foundation had high hopes he would champion their cause. They knew Clinton's brother, Roger, had done a short stretch behind bars for cocaine—before mandatory minimums were in vogue—and they noted that Attorney General Janet Reno openly questioned the need for mandatory prison terms for small, first-time dealers. But these would-be reformers did not really know their man: Bill Clinton was keenly aware that for decades Democrats had sounded more concerned about criminals than victims. Clinton thought this was stupid politics; moreover, it was not where his sympathies were. As governor of Arkansas, he had twice been burned by granting parole to lifers—only to see them murder again.

On Oct. 1, 1993, a terrible event in Petaluma, Calif., only solidified Clinton's stance on crime. At 10:30 p.m., a tattooed, bearded stranger walked through an unlocked door into, the house where a 12-year-old named Polly Klaas was having a slumber party with three of her girlfriends. The intruder, armed with a knife, tied up the other three girls and took Polly into the Northern California night. It was not until Nov. 30, when a parolee named Richard Allen Davis led police to the murder scene, that Polly's body was found. When it turned out that Davis had a lifelong history of crime, especially sexual assaults against women, grief hardened into anger. Polly's father, Marc Klaas, asked a simple question: Why was this monster even let out of prison?

The answer was that each time he'd committed a crime, Davis had quietly done his time in prison, been released and offended again in an escalating pattern of violence. Klaas devoted his life to passing three-strikes legislation, modeled after a law passed by referendum in Washington state. He found a willing audience not just in California but across the nation. Five days before Christmas 1993, Klaas met for 30 minutes with Clinton in a session that left both men emotionally drained. "Mr. President," Klaas addressed the father of a girl not much older than Polly, "let me tell you about my daughter . . . ."

A month later, during his State of the Union address, Clinton told the nation: "Those who commit crimes should be punished. And those who commit repeated, violent crimes should be told, 'When you commit a third violent crime, you will be put away, and put away for good. Three strikes, and you are out!'" It was the biggest applause line of the night. But in the end, the law signed by Clinton later that year doesn't require that all three felonies be violent crimes for the perpetrator to be put away for life. Sometimes, one will suffice. This is the great problem with sweeping laws passed in the heat of anger: There's no room for mercy or extenuating circumstances.

In 1988, for example, the mandatory minimums requirement was amended, again without much debate, to include co-conspirators or those who attempt to traffic drugs. Advertised as a tool that would help federal drug agents nab ranking members of the Medellin cartel, it has been used in practice to nab the girlfriends of petty drug dealers, occasionally for doing nothing more than telling all an informant they thought was a friend where to go to meet the boy-friend-dealer.

That's what happened in 1992 to Nicole Richardson, a 19-year-old college freshman from Mobile, Al., whose boyfriend, Jeff Thompson, was dealing LSD when Drug Enforcement Administration agents busted one of his suppliers. When a DEA informer posing as a drug buyer called his house to set up a sting, Nicole Richardson told him where Thompson could be found to pay him for the drugs. That conversation earned her a 10-year federal prison term. Her boyfriend had information of value, cooperated with authorities, got a five-year term and today is a free man. Richardson, because she knew nothing, is still inside.

Even more perverse is the way the gun "enhancements" are being used. In 1994, Monica Clyburn, a Florida welfare mom with a previous history of drug use, three small children and a baby on the way, accompanied her boyfriend to a pawnshop so they could peddle a .22-caliber pistol. Her testimony, uncontroverted by the government, was that the gun was not hers and she only filled out the required federal forms because her boyfriend did not bring his identification. Months later, when agents from the Bureau of Alcohol, Tobacco and Firearms did a routine check of records, Clyburn, who had several previous convictions on minor theft and drug charges, was arrested for being a felon in possession of a firearm. She was indicted and pleaded guilty and received the mandatory minimum of 15 years in prison. She did not use the gun to commit a crime, never even redeemed the pawnshop ticket. In other words, Clyburn had gotten *rid* of a gun—and went to prison for it.

"Everyone I've described this case to says, 'This can't be happening,'" says H. Jay Stevens, the chief federal public defender for the middle district of Florida. "The reality is that it's happening five days a week all over this country."

Second Thoughts

Such cases serve as reminders of the huge social costs associated with a policy of incarcerating 1.7 million people. One obvious cost is the burden society is incurring by tearing so many families apart. In early August, Phillip Sanders, a 43-year-old ex-con from West Palm Beach, Fla., was sentenced to life in prison under Florida's three-strikes law. His crime was shoplifting—$49.73 worth of boxer shorts and cigarette lighters, to be exact. He used a knife to cut open the packages before stuffing them down his pants and then apparently showed the knife to store employees when they confronted him in the parking lot. The local paper wrote about the case, but no one bothered to interview Sanders' two children, who will never be taken on outings with their father again.

Likewise, Monica Clyburn's four children live with their grandmother, an hour-and-45-minute drive from their mother's prison. They see, her once or twice a month, and have no father who is present in their lives. Their grandmother, Naomi Ivery, 44, of Sarasota, has high blood pressure and a family medical history that suggests this condition is a serious health risk for her. Monica's two youngest children have no memory of their mother not being behind bars. The oldest is a bright 10-year-old named Crystal, who sometimes admonishes her siblings to behave by telling them, 'If Grandma dies, where will we go?'" Ivery says Crystal is an A and B student who perhaps is too bright for her own good. "She's afraid of having to go into foster care," Ivery says. "She asks me about it all the time. I also hear her cry herself to sleep some nights; she tells me it's because she doesn't have a mother or a father here for her. God has been good to us, but I do know that these children need their mom."

The $30 billion crime bill passed in 1994 contained money for a pilot prison so that nonviolent female offenders with infants and toddlers can be housed with their children. Like most of the other prevention programs in the law, the pilot prison has not been funded, however, and the facility has never been built. In 1991, a Justice Department survey concluded that 825,000 American youths had one or both parents in prison. No research has been done since, even to determine the up-to-date number, and little is done to study these children or to help them.

Another well-documented cost is the alienation of inner-city blacks from the society at large. This can be measured in myriad ways, from chronic unemployment rates to the crisis of family formation in the black community. Often, the signs are subtle: According to the Sentencing Project, out of a total voting-age population of 10.4 million black men nationwide, nearly 1.5 million have lost the right to vote. "Voting is what makes you a citizen," observed Brenda Wright, managing attorney at the Boston-based National Voting Rights Institute.

Perhaps most ominous, as more and more young people are incarcerated, prison loses its stigma and, in fact becomes a rite of passage in certain tough communities. "I've talked to many kids, and they tell me that going to prison is like going into the Army was for the previous generation," says Barry Krisberg, president of the San Francisco-based National Council on Crime and Delinquency. "Prison doesn't scare them because almost everyone they know has been to prison."

Finally, there is the issue of money. In California, 10,000 jobs have been created in the prison system during Gov. Pete Wilson's tenure. That figure corresponds almost exactly to the number of jobs cut in the field of higher education, and punctuates one of the Rev. Jesse Jackson's more memorable rhymes: "Yale is cheaper than jail."

It's not an isolated example. According to the San Francisco-based Justice Policy Institute, state bond expenditures on prison construction in the United States surpassed those for higher education for the first time in 1995. The institute said that from 1984–92, spending per $1,000 of personal income increased less than 1 percent for higher education, while the increase for prisons was 47 percent.

In the last five years, the pressures on states to continue this trend have only mounted. Most of the billions of dollars earmarked for prison construction in the 1994 crime bill are designated only for states that require inmates to serve 85 percent of their sentences.

"We rely more on prison than we rely on early prevention, and it's a very expensive policy," says Lawrence W. Sherman, chairman of the criminal justice department at the University of Maryland. "For every piranha we're getting off the street, we're getting a lot of tuna . . . and may be turning them into piranha."

Prevention or Punishment?

Meanwhile, an increasing body of social science, rarely mentioned in Washington, is emerging that shows it's more efficient by far for government to spend money on a variety of prevention programs than on incarceration. These alternatives include after-school programs for juveniles who are unsupervised in the afternoons, family therapy for children who've exhibited aggressive behavior in school and home visits by social workers or mental health professionals to young mothers who fit various "at-risk" profiles.

Ironically, the most-conclusive of the studies showing that prevention programs pack more bang for the buck than incarceration was produced by Rand, the think tank cited as the source for the conventional wisdom that prison terms needed to be longer. Citing the recent Rand work, virtually every major law enforcement organization in the nation has called upon government to spend more for child care and after-school programs. "Political leaders are competing with each other to see who can build more prisons, but the officers who are putting people into those prisons are saying, 'We won't win this war unless we cut off the supply line,'" said Sanford A. Newman, president of a group called Fight Crime: Invest in Kids.

One has to look hard, but there are a few signs that policy-makers might be willing to re-examine what they have done. The other day, John Dilulio and former Rep. Floyd H. Flake, D-N.Y., were among the bipartisan group of leaders calling for the repeal of New York state's drug minimum statutes, known as the Rockefeller laws.

In an interview with *National Journal*, even the venerable Ed Meese, a defender of tough sentencing, conceded that the mandatories rob judges of the needed ability to temper justice with mercy in unusual cases. "It would be worthwhile to review the mandatory minimums to see if these 'horror stories' are representative or if they are very rare," Meese said. "There is very little analysis of sentencing, and that is unfortunate. I feel that any mandatory minimum needs an escape clause for use in the extraordinary case. You don't want to take all the power from the judge. . . ."

And finally, there is the testimonial of former Democratic Rep. Dan Rostenkowski of Illinois, who truly learned what he'd been voting for only after he saw the inside of prison himself after being convicted on corruption charges. He was stunned by how many low-level drug offenders were doing 15- and 20-year stretches.

"The waste of these lives is a loss to the entire community," Rostenkowski said in a May speech. "That's not a problem many people spend much time thinking about. . . . Certainly, I didn't give these issues a lot of thought when I was a member of the civilian population."

The former Ways and Means chairman went on to express his guilt for voting for these "misguided" policies. "I was swept along by the rhetoric about getting tough on crime," he said. "Frankly, I lacked both expertise and perspective on these issues. So I deferred to my colleagues who had stronger opinions but little more expertise."

Victims Against Vengeance[3]

BY FRANCIE LATOUR
BOSTON GLOBE, JUNE 18, 2000

A carjacking. A brutal murder. A son's life taken. And a father, racked by loss and seizing on a single wish: death for the killers.

The slaying of Jason Burgeson brought Ernest Burgeson and the entire town of Lakeville to life amid numbing pain, petitioning the US Department of Justice and Attorney General Janet Reno to provide a remedy the state cannot.

Rhode Island, where on June 8, Jason Burgeson and his friend Amy Shute were hijacked, shot at point-blank range, and robbed of $18, has no death penalty statute. The only chance for a death penalty outcome lies in a federal statute that elevates carjacking to a capital crime when it results in murder.

That chance, Ernest Burgeson said last week, has become his life's quest. Before a bank of cameras outside the courtroom where the alleged triggerman and four accomplices faced murder charges, he asked only to live long enough to see the alleged perpetrators—all of them—put to death.

Outrage alone does not fuel his quest.

"I just think that if they are put to death, they won't get out of jail and do this again," Burgeson said the day he buried his son. "I want to save someone else's life."

Even as overturned convictions, exonerating DNA evidence, and statewide moratoriums have led to a national soul-searching on the death penalty, Burgeson is a face and voice of the victim in the American justice system—particularly victims who lose loved ones to homicide.

In the past decade, the victims rights movement has transformed what was once a sense of powerlessness—watching some violent offenders serving fractions of their sentences, career abusers finding their way out the revolving door of a courthouse, and juveniles avoiding adult sentences for grisly crimes—into a mode of action, seeking stricter penalties and renewing calls for the death penalty. In Massachusetts, the cry for "just punishment" nearly pushed the state to reinstate the death penalty after the murder of Jeffrey Curley in 1997.

But increasingly, other faces and voices of victimhood have emerged, finding a foothold in the landscape of victims rights advocacy and challenging some of its core assumptions.

Those voices, which experts say have been overshadowed by calls for the most severe punishment, are not only publicly renouncing the death penalty, but building bridges with the offenders.

There have long been families of murder victims who privately turned away from the death penalty and dedicated themselves to alternative efforts at crime prevention.

In an unprecedented victim's plea to the court, the parents of Matthew Shepard successfully persuaded prosecutors in their son's case not to seek the death penalty.

But the fluctuating notion of what it means to be a victim reached a turning point last fall. In an unprecedented victim's plea to the court, the parents of Matthew Shepard successfully persuaded prosecutors in their son's case not to seek the death penalty.

Shepard, 21, a student at the University of Wyoming, was lashed to a wooden fence on a freezing prairie and pistol-whipped to death.

In another celebrated case, Bud Welch, whose daughter was killed in the Oklahoma City bombing, has crusaded against the death penalty, and has sat down with the father of Timothy McVeigh, convicted in the case.

And one of the most influential groups in the reconciliation movement, the Cambridge-based Murder Victims Families for Reconciliation, has brought relatives of homicide victims and relatives of violent offenders into a common conversation. Its vice chairwoman, the Rev. Renee Wormack-Keels of United Baptist Church in Jamaica Plain, lost her father to execution after he was convicted of murder, and her oldest son is serving a life sentence for murder.

In building bridges with offenders, some say Welch and others have taken on a role that should never be asked of a victim of violent crime—using the power of remorse and the possibility of reconciliation to rehabilitate offenders.

At the same time, they have stirred controversy among victims and their advocates, pointing to the death penalty as a model of vengeance that contributes to a climate of violence gripping American culture and its legal system. The United States is the only Western industrialized nation that practices capital punishment.

"I think for a long time, there was a monolithic view that all victims wanted the same thing, that all families of homicide victims have reason to want to see the death penalty," said Bonnie Bucqueroux, founder of Crime Victims for a Just Society, a Michigan-based, anti-death penalty victims group that advocates for innovative solutions to crime, including reconciliation. "But I think more and more people are starting to understand, at some point, we have to get past the part of calling for more killing and start reclaiming people. For a lot of people, using remorse to change a criminal's behavior is the only real living legacy you can have to the death of a loved one."

Bucqueroux, an early advocate of community policing, acknowledged that some have found solace in seeing a murderer executed. But she and others say many who have sought out "magic" solace—watching poison stream through the veins or electricity course through the body of a killer—have not found it.

"There is a growing awareness among victims groups that vengeance is a dead-end solution," said Bruce Shapiro, author of an upcoming book about crime victims and the politics of crime. "On the one hand, it doesn't address the anger or the grief. It leaves that wound open and at the same time it does nothing to prevent other atrocities on a broad scale."

With the exception of the Shepard case, Shapiro said, victims and survivors who ask the legal system not to pursue the death penalty are routinely disregarded. And among the broader society, there is a stigma—sometimes silent, sometimes vocal—that accuses victims who don't seek the maximum punishment of not loving those they lost enough.

"I think what we're seeing nationally is the rise of victims who . . . will not settle for a narrow view of what politicians or the media say being a victim means," Shapiro said.

"There is a growing awareness among victims groups that vengeance is a dead-end solution."— **Bruce Shapiro, author**

Walter Everett turned the notion of what it means to be a victim on its head: Four years after he watched his son's killer, Michael Carlucci, sentenced in court, he spoke before a parole board supporting his early release.

Four years later, Everett, a Hartford pastor, officiated at Carlucci's wedding. Now, he and Carlucci, a supervisor at a trucking company, are good friends who eat together regularly and speak around the country about their decade-long journey.

The killer who robbed Everett of ever officiating at his own son's wedding has not strayed back to crime. But Everett said that when he began to reach out to Carlucci, other victims who had lost loved ones to homicide shunned him.

"It was though I had betrayed the group," Everett said of the survivors support group he was attending at the time.

He could understand the anger and grief that gripped other survivors for years, Everett said. But he said the anger was debilitating him, victimizing him twice over, and he felt strongly he had to release it.

"I had moved in a direction that they did not want to go in," he said of other victims he encountered. "It was isolating."

Paul G. Cassell, a law professor at the University of Utah, who testifies on the rights of crime victims, said that while more have begun to seek remedies like Everett's, they remain in the minority. The approach of reconciliation and confronting offenders, he said, remains most common where the offenders have committed lesser crimes, and among juveniles.

"I think the most important thing is that there should never be a one-size-fits-all model for how to be a victim," Cassell said. "More than anything, victims want their voices heard. Whether they seek just punishment in the death penalty or forgiveness is less important than that their voices be heard and respected."

III. Bars of Gold:
Prison Economics

Editor's Introduction

T
he United States' $45 billion per year correctional budget benefits a host of companies that supply goods and services for America's prisons, including private corporations that are paid by state governments to house inmates. In addition, many companies, including Microsoft, Honda, Victoria's Secret, and TWA, employ prison labor, a practice that has provoked complaints from job seekers about lost opportunities and unfair competition. Depressed communities, mostly in rural areas, have stimulated their economies by building prisons, perhaps most notably in New York's North Country (the northernmost region of the state), where approximately one out of 20 people is serving time.

Section III offers several different perspectives on the connection between money and the American prison system. In "Public-Private Partnerships in the U.S. Prison System," Anne Larason Schneider looks at the history, claims, and issues surrounding private prisons, which are for-profit, publicly traded correctional facilities run by private corporations. As she discusses the prisoner "market," Schneider says, "Private-sector involvement in prison policy adds significant new target populations to the political arena by introducing businesses, corporations, and stockholders in publicly traded private prisons into the lobbying milieu." Schneider concludes that neither private- nor government-run prisons are likely to hold permanent sway because both are doomed to fall under repeated criticism from the media, the public, and politicians.

Complimenting Schneider's analysis of private prisons, Joseph T. Hallinan, in "Private Prisons Not Saving," reports that, though they have enjoyed great expansion since the 1980s, these companies have not reduced costs to the extent promised, according to a report by the General Accounting Office. Stock prices of many private-prison companies have fallen or are leveling off.

In "Crime and Punishment" Cait Murphy appraises the prison system from a financial standpoint. She finds that incarcerating criminals is fiscally advisable only up to a certain point. While presenting a cost analysis, she argues that nonviolent drug offenders should be enrolled in drug treatment programs. Furthermore, she suggests that the benefits of prison rehabilitation programs, such as job training and education, outweigh the costs.

Public-Private Partnerships in the U.S. Prison System[1]

BY ANNE LARASON SCHNEIDER*
AMERICAN BEHAVIORAL SCIENTIST, SEPTEMBER 1999

Public-private partnerships in the operation of prisons have existed from the colonial period to contemporary times, although the extent of reliance on the private sector and the policy design models have varied somewhat. Drawing on ideas from policy design theory (Schneider & Ingram, 1997), this study will identify the characteristics of the partnerships, the reasons for private-sector involvement, the rationales and claims made by competing perspectives, and the consequences of private-sector involvement.[1]

Prison policy differs from other policy arenas in ways that have implications for the appropriate role of the private sector. First, prisons deliver punishment, whereas most policies deliver benefits or regulations. Other policies that impose costs—such as tax policy—may be unwanted or resented, but no other policy arena actually delivers punishment. Second, the target populations of prison policy are vastly different from most target populations—prisoners are not free, they do not make choices about most events in their daily life, they have virtually no political power, and they are socially constructed as deviant or violent by most of the population. Third, although many policy arenas offer some form of political capital for elected officials, few, if any, offer such lucrative possibilities as prisons.[2] By inflicting harsh punishment upon criminals who are socially constructed as deviant, violent, and undeserving, elected officials can gain the accolades of the general public without incurring any noticeable political costs from those actually receiving the punishment. The monetary costs of mandatory long sentences are postponed to the future and spread across all taxpayers. Thus, it may be many years after legislation is passed before the full financial impact is felt. Finally, private-sector involvement in prison policy adds significant new target populations to the political arena by introducing businesses, corporations, and stockholders in publicly

1. Anne Larason Schneider, *American Behavioral Scientist* (Vol. 43, No. 1) pp. 192–208, copyright © 1999 by Sage Publications, Inc. Reprinted by permission of Sage Publications, Inc.

* Author's Note: The author would like to acknowledge the valuable information provided by Terry Stewart, Director of the Arizona Department of Corrections. All points of view and interpretations of data, of course, are those of the author.

traded private prisons into the lobbying milieu. These groups have much to gain from a continued expansion of the number of prisoners available—that is, the prisoner "market."

Because of these differences, the politics of policy making may take on different characteristics, and the criteria by which policy should be evaluated must go beyond the usual reliance on effectiveness or efficiency to include the contributions of policy to justice, citizenship, and democratic institutions. It is one question to ask whether private involvement in prison management is more efficient on a per prisoner basis, but quite another question to ask whether the number of prisoners in society as a whole is efficient, or just, or appropriate in other ways for a democratic society.

The Rise and Decline of Public-Private Prison Partnerships

The three following basic types of partnerships have been apparent in the history of prisons in the United States: ownership of the facility in which the prisoners are kept; private use of prison labor and taking of profits from their labor; and private management of the facility, including the day-by-day supervision of prisoners.

Case studies of the emergence of prisons in the American states suggest that private involvement began through a convergence of interests among reformers, public officials, and local businesses (Shichor, 1995; Walker, 1980). Humanitarian reformers believed that prisons would be more humane than common forms of punishment in the American colonies—and later in the western frontier—which were death, branding, torture, or other physical punishment. The role of reformers was evident in the founding of the first prison in the Quaker colony of William Penn when the great law of 1682 banned the death penalty for everything except premeditated murder. This prison was a 5 feet by 7 feet cell. Later, the colony rented space from local businesses (Walker, 1980).

Public officials from the colonial period to the early 1900s believed that prisons could be self-supporting or even profitable for the state, and businesses were interested in sharing in those profits. Some states permitted a private individual or firm to build, manage, and handle the day-to-day operation of the prison itself, a system similar to the ones that have generated such intense debate in the 1980s and 1990s. Knepper (1990) reports that in 1825, Kentucky was not making enough money to support its growing prison population and was in desperate financial straits. A businessman, Joel Scott, paid the state $1,000 a year for the work of convicts in a 250-bed facility that he built and operated, with all profits kept for his own company.

In Louisiana (Walker, 1980), the state leased out the entire operation for 5 years and received $50,000 for the lease. Tennessee, in 1866, leased its Nashville prison to a furniture company for 43 cents per day per prisoner, reportedly because it was suffering from severe financial difficulties, and the number of prisoners had greatly expanded after the Civil War ended. California, in 1851, could not keep up with the increased crime attributed to the influx of settlers and was close to bankruptcy (Shichor, 1995), so the state leased its prison for 10 years to two local businessmen.

Oklahoma and Arizona not only viewed the prisons as potential profitmaking entities for the state and for local businesses, but considered prisons to be an important part of the state's economic development program (Conley, 1980, 1981; Knepper, 1990). Oklahoma prisoners actually built McAlister Prison, which included an industrial factory and a 2,000-acre farm. Arizona's first territorial governor, Anson P. K. Safford, believed that a territorial prison would show that the territory was civilized and had a stable social environment sufficient to attract eastern businesses (Knepper, 1990). He was able to exploit the racial characteristics of prisoners—claiming that most of them were wild and dangerous Mexicans who preyed on travelers throughout the state, especially near the Mexican border. He also claimed that it would be the first profit-making state institution and that hard work was good for the health of prisoners (Knepper,1990). Arizona eventually contracted with a private firm, the Arizona Canal Company, to take over the entire daytime operation of the prison. The prison provided all male convicts to the company for 10 years, for 70 cents per day, in the form of future water rights.

All of these forms of public-private partnerships eventually generated serious problems that produced opposition from business, labor, and humanitarian reformers. In some states, prisoners rioted or protested to such an extent that the partnerships were ended. For example, Tennessee ended its lease arrangement only a year after it began, apparently because the inmates burned the furniture factory. Subsequently, they built branch prisons and leased the prisoners to coal mining companies. In 1891 and 1892, free miners raided the prisons and set the prisoners free, reportedly because the competition was hurting them economically (Knepper,1990). In Alabama, Knepper reported that opponents were worried that private leasing of prison labor would undermine the fundamental principle of restoring the prisoner's sense of obligation to a just society. They were worried that lessees would try to lengthen the sentences of good workers by giving bad reports about them.

Humanitarian reformers in Texas focused on what they viewed as excessive inmate deaths and injuries that were blamed on the private companies and the prisons they operated. California's contract system was accused of bid rigging, having a corrupt trustee system, selling of pardons, and other issues to the point that the Governor physically took control of San Quentin from the lessee—a former member of the legislature—and used the scandal for political advantage (Shichor, 1995). After a court had ruled that the takeover was illegal, the state had to buy the lease back from the private company for $275,000. In Oklahoma, businesses that did not have contracts joined with labor unions to oppose the prison industry system on the grounds of unfair competition (Conley, 1981).

New York passed legislation in 1842 that restricted the use of prison labor so much that it essentially ended public-private partnerships, and by the turn of the century, most other states had followed suit. Finally, in 1935, the social reform legislation initiated by the Roosevelt administration produced the Hawes-Cooper Act that

---

By the beginning of World War II, public-private partnerships in prisons were virtually nonexistent.

---

authorized states to prohibit the entry of prison-made goods produced in other states. In 1936, the Walsh-Healy Act prohibited convict labor on government contracts that exceeded $10,000. In 1940, the Sumners-Ashurst Act made it a federal offense to transport prison-made goods across state borders, regardless of state laws. By the beginning of World War II, public-private partnerships in prisons were virtually nonexistent.

The Reemergence of Public-Private Partnerships: Private Prisons

Although prison industries have enjoyed a small resurgence, the most discussed form of public-private partnership today is the one popularly called private prisons, in which a private firm operates (and usually owns) a secure adult facility for prisoners and solicits contracts with local, state, or federal governments.[3]

These relationships are different and far more complex than those in the previously discussed historical period. The 19th century experiments with private involvement almost always involved local businesses. In the 1990s, the businesses are national and international corporations—some of which are publicly traded on one or another of the major stock exchanges. Although some of the private prisons have emerged as a result of contracts with the state in which they are located, the more common situation is that a private firm builds a prison in a state and simultaneously attempts to negotiate contracts with the home state—or any other state, county, or federal entity—for prisoners. The firm is usually paid on a per diem basis, either on the number of prisoners it houses for a particular entity or on the number of places it has reserved for that jurisdiction. In the past, the business paid the state for use of its prisoners; today, the state pays the business to manage the prisoners. Some state contracts, such as Arizona's, require that the Department of Corrections place a monitor on site to make critical decisions about disciplinary matters. Most of the state contracts require that private firms offer the service at 5% to 10% below what it would have cost the state. This, of course, creates complicated cost models involving a delicate balancing act between accounting principles and political realities. In Arizona and some other states, the state law actually includes a detailed description of what is to be counted

---

The number of places for prisoners in private facilities has increased from 1,345 (0.5% of all prisoners) in 1985 to 106,940 (8.5% of all prisoners) by December 1997.

---

or not counted in the costs of both private and public prisons (Prison Privatization Act, 1998). Arizona legislation requires that private prisons take out large insurance policies to reimburse state agencies that may have to intervene when an escape is in process or a riot occurs.

The growth of private prisons has been dramatic, as the number of places for prisoners in private facilities has increased from 1,345 (0.5% of all prisoners) in 1985 to 106,940 (8.5% of all prisoners) by December 1997 (Thomas, Bolinger, & Badalamenti, 1998). Thomas, Bolinger, and Badalamenti's *Private Adult Correctional Facility Census*, 10th edition (1997), listed 118 facilities located in 25 different states and Washington, DC; Puerto Rico; Australia; and the United Kingdom. The Private Prison Project at the University of Florida currently shows 162 facilities with 132,346 places (Thomas, 1999). Texas has 19 private prisons, the most of any state by far, as well as having the largest prison capacity and the highest number of actual prisoners held. Most of these prisoners, however, are not from Texas. In 1997, almost 6,000 prisoners from 14 different states were "outsourced" from their home state to a private prison located elsewhere. Most of the privately managed facilities are in the South (with 74, 41% of the total); this is followed by the West (with 32, 27% of the total). There are only 5 in the midwestern states, and only 1 of these has contracts that permit it to take prisoners from the state where it is located. There are only 4 in the Northeast, and none has contracts with its home state. The 5 facilities in the Northeast take local prisoners, federal prisoners, and out-of-state prisoners.

Subgovernment Politics and the Growth of Private Prisons

The Corrections Corporation of America (CCA) was the first corporation to enter the private prison business and currently is the largest one. In 1998, CCA officially became Prison Realty Corporation, and it, along with 10 other private prison businesses, is traded on a major stock exchange. The emergence of CCA is well worth describing here, for it is indeed a new model of public-private partnership in the prison business and it offers a fascinating case of subgovernment policy making.

CCA was well connected with political and financial leaders in Tennessee, and it had strong ties to experts in the prison business. One of the founders of Nashville-based CCA was Tom Beasley, a former chair of the Tennessee Republican party, and another was Nashville banker and financier, Doctor R. Crants. Another CCA founder, Don Hutton, was the former head of the American Correctional Association—the association responsible for the accreditation standards of adult prisons (Shichor, 1995). Several high-ranking political officials in Tennessee owned CCA stock, including Honey Alexander (wife of the Governor, Lamar Alexander); the state insurance commissioner, John Neff; and the Speaker of the House of Representatives, Ned McWherter. He and Mrs. Alexander both divested themselves of CCA shares to avoid conflict of interest (Shichor,1995; American Federation of State, County, and Municipal Employees [AFSCME], 1998).

In 1985, Tennessee reportedly faced a crisis in its criminal justice system (Folz & Scheb, 1989). The state was under a court order to reduce the number of prisoners from 7,700 to 7,019 within 3 months. The previous year, they had the highest rate of inmate-on-inmate violence of any state in the union. To complicate the situation further, Tennessee faced a significant budget shortfall and a rate of 450 new prison admissions for every 250 releases.

Realizing that Tennessee faced this kind of pressure, CCA offered to pay the state $100 million for a 99-year lease to operate the entire adult correctional system. CCA reportedly offered to invest $250 million in new facilities, and to receive $170 million per year to manage the system, which was approximately the size of the current state budget for prisons. According to the case study by Folz and Scheb (1989), Republican Governor Lamar Alexander was very interested, and it appeared that bipartisan support for privatization was substantial. A public opinion poll showed that 40% of the voters favored it, with 32% disapproving. Intense lobbying, however, scuttled the CCA proposal, with the most active opposition from the Tennessee State Employees Association; Tennessee Bar Association; Tennessee Trial Layers; American Civil Liberties Union; and AFSCME (AFSCME, 1998).

A much more modest bill was adopted during the 1986 session and signed into law, permitting private management of one new medium security facility. The restrictions written into this bill, however, were so unfavorable to business that there was only one firm bid on it (CCA declined). The first state contract in Tennessee was not granted until 1992 (to CCA), during the administration of Governor Ned McWherter, who was elected governor after Alexander. This contract was immediately challenged on conflict-of-interest grounds because another firm, U.S. Corrections Corporation, reportedly had submitted a lower bid (AFSCME, 1998).

CCA also contacted Texas officials in 1984 (Ethridge, 1990). Ethridge, in his doctoral dissertation, reports that Governor Mark White, a Democrat, viewed the private prison possibility as an opportunity to direct some business to a particular group of developers, and after CCA agreed to use those developers, White reportedly assisted CCA in gaining financial support from Merrill Lynch. Criticism about his close ties to the developers was deflected, Ethridge reports, by White's claim that private prisons were part of his economic development program for the state. CCA promised, among other things, a 20% savings in the costs of prison construction and operation. The legislation was passed with bipartisan support, according to Ethridge, although it was not passed until after White had left office and was succeeded by Bill Clements.

The policy-making context in Texas also was described as one of crisis and failed criminal justice policy (Ethridge, 1990). The total admissions to prison in Texas were twice the number of releases (Ethridge), the state had been found in contempt of court for not having obeyed previous orders to reduce overcrowding, Governor Clements reportedly faced a $231 million budget deficit for fiscal year 1986, and the estimates were that $400 million was needed to build enough prisons to meet the court mandate. The only person to speak against the legislation was the legislative coordinator for the Texas State Employee Union (Ethridge), who said that it was morally wrong and involved a fundamental conflict of interest because profit motives were not consistent with the best interests of prisons and the public. He was quoted as follows:

> Because prison contracts are structured on a per diem basis, the interests of the corporation will be to increase occupancy rates, to increase profits. . . . There is also a conflict of interest because

corporate correctional officers will seek to maintain an ever increasing incarceration population and will lobby for tougher prison sentencing policies. (Ethridge, p. 82)

In 1987, Texas took the additional step of passing legislation that permitted local governments to contract for private facilities without having a vote of the people, which ordinarily would be required for any capital project. This may have contributed to the fact that Texas now has more private facilities (19) than any other state.

> *In 1987, Texas took the ... step of passing legislation that permitted local governments to contract for private facilities without having a vote of the people.*

Privatization has also sparked old-fashioned partisan politics in some states. Arizona's Republican-controlled legislature passed legislation authorizing private prisons in 1985 and again in 1986, but both bills were vetoed by Democratic Governor Bruce Babbitt. Another bill was passed in 1987 and signed by Republic Governor, Evan Mecham, but Arizona's public employee union filed suit against the legislation on constitutional grounds and won. Republican-controlled legislatures again passed privatization legislation in 1988 that was vetoed by Democratic Governor Rose Mofford, who had taken over as Governor after the impeachment of Evan Mecham. Privatization legislation finally succeeded in 1990, when it was approved mainly along party lines in the legislature and signed into law by Republican Governor Fife Symington. The partisan nature of private involvement in prisons is also documented by Gallagher and Edwards (1997), who found that states with Democratic governors and strong labor unions were more resistant to private prison industries.

The private prison subgovernment not only includes business leaders, state-elected officials, political party elites, and correctional experts, but also two influential social science researchers as well. The initial studies by both Logan and Thomas indicated that privatization had reduced the costs of prisons (Logan, 1990, 1996; Logan & McGriff, 1989; Thomas, 1997). Thomas is a member of CCA's Prison Realty Corporation's board of directors, and his center at the University of Florida had been partially funded by the corporation (Thomas, 1999). Academics on the whole have been very cautious about the privatization of prisons, if not opposed to it (McDonald, 1990; Shichor, 1995; Sparks, 1994); thus, the emergence of research by well-respected academics that shows private prisons to be less expensive or higher quality has been important in legitimizing the arguments presented by businesses and policy makers.

The Rhetoric, Claims, and Script of Private Prisons

The most common script offered as an explanation for the growth of private prisons is that increasing crime rates, along with mandatory sentences and longer terms, have produced a rapid increase in prisoners. The increase in prisoners produced extensive overcrowding in secure adult facilities during the 1980s—a time when almost all states were faced with serious financial problems and budget deficits.

> *The increase in prisoners is accounted for by public policy changes, not changes in the propensity of people to inflict harm on others.*

These factors created a crisis in criminal justice policy, and public officials turned to the private sector to reduce the costs of prison operation.

As plausible as this scenario seems, it is simply inaccurate in some respects. There has been a virtual explosion in the number of persons sentenced to secure state and federal facilities, but it is very difficult to sustain an argument that the increase in prisoners has been the logical result of people committing more crimes than in the past. Data on the rate of imprisonment from 1925 to 1973 show that there was virtually no change in the rate of imprisonment, with the rate hovering around 100 prisoners per 100,000 people (Schneider, 1998). From 1973 to 1997, however, the rate increased to an all-time high of 446 prisoners per 100,000 people (Bureau of Justice Statistics, 1998; Maguire & Pastore, 1994, 1996). If this were produced by an increase in crime, then one would expect the rate of crime commission to have increased in a similar way, but, except for drug crimes, this is not the case. In fact, victimization survey data on commission of violent crimes has been going down, not up, since 1973 when the first victimization survey was conducted (Maguire & Pastore, 1994). The uniform crime data on murder, which is the most serious and the most precise in terms of definition, shows an up-and-down pattern, certainly not a steady upward trend that could in any way account for the increase in prisoners (Bureau of Justice Statistics, 1998; Maguire & Pastore, 1995).

The increase in prisoners is accounted for by public policy changes, not changes in the propensity of people to inflict harm on others. The policy changes that produced the increase in incarceration and the overcrowding that results include longer sentences, mandatory sentences, three strikes you're out, no parole, no early release, and the huge increase in penalties for drug offenses. The point here is that turning to the private sector to build more prisons or to manage prisons so that the savings can be used to offset deficits, reduce overcrowding, or permit even more growth in incarceration is a policy choice made by elected public officials. There were other choices that could have been made. By the end of 1996, only 18 states had authorized contracts for private prisons within their state, and 32 had not. It must be emphasized that most states cannot prevent a private business from building a prison in the state and contracting with the federal government or with other states to take their prisoners. Unless a state passes legislation prohibiting the prison business, it is subject to finding one of these within its borders at some point in the future.

The policy choices available to states that are alternatives to privatization include reducing the scope of incarcerative sanctions, increasing the number of community-based alternatives, reducing the length of sentences, increasing the number of early release programs, or investing in prevention programs such as early childhood parenting and education.

The second part of the script is that the increase in prisoners produced overcrowding (which is supported by the evidence), and that overcrowding, combined with tight budgets, led public officials to turn to the private sector to build or manage prisons with the promise of a 5% to 20% savings. This savings, presumably, would permit the state to reduce its overcrowding. To examine this claim, I conducted an analysis in which the number of private prison contracts in the state is regressed on the three following possible explanatory variables: the extent of budget health from 1980 to 1986 (as measured by the difference between revenue one year and expenditures the next year, divided by expenditures; see Berry & Berry, 1992), the extent of overcrowding in the state and local prison systems, and the rate of incarceration (Schneider, 1998). The first two variables reflect the expectation that privatization was produced by the combination of an overcrowded prison system and the budget shortfalls characteristic of the 1980 to 1986 period. The third variable, rate of incarceration per 100,000, is a commonly used indicator for the punitiveness of the criminal justice system in the state.

The results show that budget health is statistically significant, but in the opposite direction of the prediction (beta = .36, t = 2.64, significance = .012). That is, states with larger budget shortfalls were less likely to turn to the private sector. Overcrowding had no significant relationship (beta = -.089, t = -.66). On the other hand, states with higher rates of incarceration were more likely to have private prison contracts (beta = .32, t = 2.4, significance = .02). The conclusion I draw is that increased privatization was driven by the same kinds of value orientations that produce more punitive criminal justice systems—a generalized sort of conservative, antigovernment, law-and-order ideology.

The purpose of this paper is not to offer a complete predictive model of the growth of private prisons, but only to examine the efficacy of the rationales that have been offered. Increases in the number of prisoners, overcrowding, and tight budgets were not causal factors that forced states to turn to private prison management. Instead, these trends required the states to confront the punitiveness of the criminal justice policies that had been produced in the decades after the 1960s. These trends established a context within which privatization could be promoted as a solution to a problem. In Kingdon's (1984) terms, it opened a window of opportunity in which a solution (privatization) found the problem that it could help solve.

In Schneider and Ingram's (1993, 1997) framework, privatization gave policy makers the opportunity to gain political capital through the appearance of doing something about the failed criminal justice system and simultaneously open up market opportunities for private business. It offered the attractive political opportunity to continue the negative social construction of prisoners and, at the same time, to develop a new positively constructed constituency of businesses, corporations, and stockholders who could profit from prisons. Support for private prisons also permitted officials to take advantage of the positive valance associated with downsizing government through privatization.

Policy makers in some states turned to privatization, others did not—at least not yet. The rationales used in states that adopted privatization could have been used with just as much credibility, if not more credibility, in states that resisted the privatization movement.

Issues, Costs, and Quality of Public-Private Partnerships

The media coverage of private prisons has tended toward the dramatic, and it is usually unfavorable. More than one state has had the experience of a riot or escape from a private prison within its borders that houses persons who are from other states entirely. Local police and state highway patrol are expected to help quell the riot or find the escapees—at public expense. Ohio discovered that a private prison within its borders was taking prisoners classified as maximum security when they thought that the prison had agreed to only take minimum and medium security prisoners. However, these kinds of problems—riots, escapes, inmate-on-inmate violence—also occur in publicly managed prisons, and there have been far too few studies making reliable comparisons to draw the conclusion that private prisons are more subject to these sorts of problems than public prisons.

Most of the empirical research on private prisons emphasizes cost differences. Although fraught with methodological problems, the current studies are summarized in Table 1. For the most part, these studies show a slight advantage to the private prisons and illustrate (in Texas, at least) that a state may realize a reduction in per inmate cost, over time. It is interesting to note, however, that comparative data are available for only a handful of the private prisons. Following are some of the many methodological issues:

How should indirect costs be allocated in the public and private facilities? Should the cost of the private and public facilities be

---

For the most part . . . studies show a slight advantage to the private prisons and illustrate (in Texas, at least) that a state may realize a reduction in per inmate cost, over time.

---

based on the actual average daily population or on the number of places the facility is built to hold? What should be done if it is more than 100% full?

Should the state costs associated specifically with privatization (e.g., having monitors on site) be counted as part of the cost of the private prison? Should in-kind services provided by one public agency to another be added to the cost of the public prison (e.g., health or mental health programs)? Should services provided by the public sector to the private prison, such as capturing escapees or prosecuting inmates for violent acts on one another, be added to the private prison's costs?

Should the taxes paid by private prisons be adjusted out, as Thomas (1997) has done in his cost studies, on the grounds that these are returned to the state?

In addition, the studies virtually never explain how or why the private prison manages to have lower costs even though they have the added responsibility of making a profit. There is a general perception that the reduced costs are at the expense of employee salaries. The methodologies also suffer because the comparisons, due to necessity, are of only one or two institutions and usually cover only 1 year of data. The natural variability in annual expenditures for

Table 1: Summary of Cost Studies

State	Cost per Inmate per Day		Year (data)	Comment
	Private	Public		
Texas	$36.76	$42.70 to $43.13	1990	Study conducted by the Texas Sunset Advisory Commission compared four private prerelease minimum security prisons for males with hypothetical operation by the state (operational costs only)
	$33.95 to $33.61	$39.79 to $38.64	1995 to 1996	Texas Criminal Justice Policy Council report to the legislature in January 1997, for prisoners in the Texas Institutional Division (reported in Thomas, 1998)
	$27.91	$28.96	1996	Texas Criminal Justice Policy Council report to the legislature in January 1997, for prisoners in the Texas Jail Division (reported in Thomas, 1998)
California	$42.67	$36.15 to $45.55	1991 to 1992	Sechrest and Shichor (1993) compared three for-profit community correctional facilities, one operated by a private business, one by a local government, and one by a police department, both of the latter on a for-profit basis under contract from the state
Tennessee	$73.50	$77.50	1985 to 1988	Logan and McGriff (1989) compared two privately operated 350-bed facilities in Hamilton County, Tennessee (these cost figures assume full occupancy)
	$35.39	$34.90 to $35.45	1993 to 1994	Tennessee Select Oversight Committee on Corrections, 1995, studied one private, minimum-maximum security facility for men with two similar public facilities (U.S. GAO report considers this study to have the best methodology)
Washington (Tennessee data)	$33.61	$35.82 to $35.28	1993 to 1994	Washington's Department of Corrections Privatization Feasibility Study (Legislative Budget Committee for the State of Washington, 1996) used the same data from the Tennessee study of 1993 to 1994, but adjusted it as if the facilities were at full capacity
(Louisiana data)	$23.75 to $23.34	$23.55	1995 to 1996	Washington's Department of Corrections Privatization Feasibility Study (Legislative Budget Committee for the State of Washington, 1996) compared two private and one public mixed-custody facilities in Louisiana
Louisiana				Archambeault and Deis (1996; quoted in Thomas, 1998) compared three large medium-maximum security prisons in Louisiana over 5 fiscal years, 1992 to 1996, and found cost savings of 11.7% for the 5-year totals
Arizona	$35.90 to $44.37	$43.08	1995 to 1996	Thomas's (1997) study of Arizona's costs produced an estimate of $44.37 for a private, 450-bed dual gender minimum security prison (Marana) when taking into account the state officials located at the site, but arrived at an adjusted cost of $35.90 after amortizing the costs of constructions, not including the taxes paid by the facility and other adjustments

any particular prison may be rather high from one year to the next, and differences as simple as the average age (experience) of employees may account for sizable cost differences between institutions.

Quality comparisons are even less common than cost analyses, although there have been some researchers who have made concerted efforts to develop a methodology with solid theoretical underpinnings for quality studies. Logan (1996) compared a New Mexico women's prison, operated under private contract with the prison that had previously housed New Mexico's women inmates, with a federal women's prison in West Virginia. He examined eight dimensions of service (security, safety, order, care, activity, justice, conditions, and management), each with six or eight separate indicators. The data included staff and inmate surveys as well as institutional records. He concluded that the private prison, overall, had a higher level of service quality, even though there were some interesting differences between staff and inmate assessments (with staff preferring the private prison and inmates preferring the public one).

Thomas' (1997) study of Arizona included several qualitative comparisons, but the fact that the private facility (Marana) housed a mixed gender population made comparisons risky. On most of the indicators, there were no differences, mainly because the time periods were so short that some of the more serious kinds of incidents (riots, inmate-on-inmate assaults or murders, staff abuse of prisoners) were not reported from any facility. The privately operated facility (Marana) had fewer jobs assigned per inmate than the medium security (level 2) public prisons (52 compared with 83), and was given lower ratings by the state's annual audits on most of the indicators. The private prison had an overall good rating, whereas all of the public facilities received an overall excellent rating. It is impossible to know whether these audit data reflect real differences in performance or system bias against private prisons.

Lanza-Kaduce, Parker, and Thomas (1999) conducted a comparative recidivism analysis for the Florida state legislature in which they compared the 12-month recidivism records of persons released from two privately operated facilities and those released from public facilities. The research design involved a sample matched-on-offense category (using 53 specific categories), race, number of prior incarcerations, and age. Multiple measures of recidivism were used, including rearrest, reconviction, and resentencing to incarceration as well as an overall indicator of any recidivism. There was a sample size of 198 in each group. With fewer rearrests (96 compared to 192), fewer reincarcerations (101 to 146), and fewer incidents of any form (172 to 237), the results clearly gave the edge to private facilities. There were similar differences in the severity of the recidivism offense. Finally, the study compared persons in the private facility who had completed their assigned programs and those who had not. The lower recidivism rates in the private prison, compared to the public prison, were due almost entirely to the fact that the private facility had more persons who completed their assigned rehabilitative programs. The noncompleters had recidivism rates almost identical to the persons from the public facilities—giving some powerful indication that successful completion of in-prison programs predicts the reduction of subsequent criminal activity.

A study of several Louisiana prisons (Archambeault & Deis, 1996) included a number of qualitative dimensions. The state-operated facilities were found to have higher quality in terms of preventing escapes, preventing sexual offenses, using urine testing, and having a wide scope of educational and job-related programs. The private facilities were found to have fewer critical incidents, a safer work environment for employees and prisoners, more effective discipline, and better access to programs for prisoners.

The design and methodologies of these studies indicate that on a localized, institutional basis, private prisons appear not to damage or harm the criminal justice system capacity of the state, and it may reduce costs without reducing service, or it may even improve service.

Another empirical question that needs analysis is whether public-private partnerships accentuate the pressure for an ever-increasing supply of prisoners, leading to longer sentences and more intrusive criminal justice practices. It would be naive to believe that private prison corporations are not involved in lobbying, and it would be equally naive to expect that they are only interested in capturing a larger market share from the public-sector prisons. In fact, possible conflicts between the two can be avoided if both work to ensure that there is a ready supply of prisoners to be housed. Prison as the punishment of choice has always been politically attractive, but it is limited due to its long-term cost. Even though the public may be easily swayed by the law and order rhetoric into believing that long prison terms are deserved by those who break the law, the public, nevertheless, does not like to spend money on people they perceive as undeserving, such as prisoners and would prefer to allocate those funds to education or other target populations. Hence, public-private partnerships that permit a large role for the private sector have the potential effect of bringing about a coalition between public and private providers of prisons with both advocating for increasing the scope of duration of prison sentences. Second, private management appears to cost less and therefore can be promoted by elected officials as a way of reducing the costs of the criminal justice system, even though the number of persons imprisoned stays the same or even increases.

The results of a regression analysis (see Schneider, 1998) indicate weak supports for these contentions, although the newness of private prisons and the complexities of the policy-making process are such that caution is in order. The results show that states with more contracts to private prison companies within their jurisdiction in 1996 had higher rates of incarceration per 100,000 in 1997 than states with fewer contracts (beta = .50, t = 3.85, significance = .000), even when budget health was controlled. This conclusion should be taken with caution, however, because the proportion of all prisoners who could be held in private facilities currently under contract or being built is still only about 8%. Furthermore, the time lag in the causal analysis is complicated. Decisions by a state to permit private prisons occur through several legislative sessions and may not result in any private prison contracts for several years after the authorization. The incarceration rate is the product of policy decisions over a long period of time, not simply during 1 year. It is possible that the rate of incarceration and the use of private contracts are both the product of an underlying conservative ideology, but it is also possible that political dynamics are being altered by the presence of private prisons in the state in such a way that the state can continue to increase the proportion of its population it is able and willing to place behind bars.

> *Extensive private involvement will give way to public delivery mechanisms that, in turn, will yield to private ones at some future time.*

Conclusions and Implications

Public-private partnerships in prison operation is different from most other policy arenas because prisons deliver punishment, and there is no way to turn this into a technical administrative exercise devoid of discretion. When private owners or managers run a prison, they hire the guards and staff, and set the tone for how the prisoners are treated. There is enormous discretion exercised by the caseworkers who are in direct contact with prisoners. There are important differences between delivering service, benefits, treatment, or regulations to a target population and delivering confinement, orders, rules, discipline, and physical pain to a captive population that has no choice and no say in how they are treated.

In terms of the future of public-private partnerships in prisons, I believe this is a policy arena in which we would expect to find pendulum effects similar to those observed during historical experiments with private involvement. Extensive private involvement will give way to public delivery mechanisms that, in turn, will yield to private ones at some future time. A pendulum pattern in public and private delivery systems is expected because prisons are institutions that cannot be managed as effectively as expected by the media, political elites, or general public regardless of whether they are entirely under government control or whether they involve extensive privatization. Perhaps prisons will never be effective enough in producing public safety because public safety is more contingent on societal factors, such as families, communities, schools, nonprofits, economic opportunities, and the absence of race and class discrimination. Institutions that cannot produce the level of performance expected and desired by the media, political leaders, and the public will move from the public sector toward partnerships with extensive private involvement, and then back toward the public sector, as the private gives up on them.

Notes

1. First, policy design theory emphasizes the substance of policy. What is being delivered to whom using what kinds of tools (incentives), with what rules, through which implementation structures, with what goals in mind (both symbolic and instrumental), with what rationales, and with what kinds of underlying assumptions. Second, policy design theory recognizes that policies emerge from a complex context involving the dynamic interplay between political power, social constructions (of events, people, facts), and the rationales that are used to justify various policy choices. Third, our theory of policy design posits the following four evaluative criteria for public policy: efficient problem solving, justice, citizenship, and democratic institutions. Policy design theory is intended to integrate interpretive (constructivist) perspectives with explanatory (positive) perspectives. Because this paper is intended mainly to analyze a particular kind of public-private partnership, the approach will reflect the theoretical underpinnings but not emphasize theory.
2. Political capital refers to the ability of elected officials to manipulate a policy arena to enhance their potential for reelection or election to higher office.
3. For a discussion of the reemergence of prison industries, see the lengthier version of this paper, Schneider, 1998.

References

American Federation of State, County, and Municipal Employees (1998). *Corrections Corporation of America Public Employee*, January, February [On-line]. Available: *http://www.afscme.org/afscme/press/pejf9809.html.*

Archambeault, W. G., & Deis, D. R., Jr. (1996). *Private versus public prisons in Louisiana*. Report to the National Institute of Justice [On-line]. Available: *http://www.uss.uconn.edu/~wwwsoci*.

Berry, E. S., & Berry, W. D. (1992). Tax innovation in the states: Capitalizing on political opportunity. *American Journal of Political Science, 36*, 715–742.

Bureau of Justice Statistics. (1998). *Prisoners and prison capacity* [On-line]. Available: *http://www.ojp.usdog.gov/bjs/pub*.

Conley, J. A. (1980). Revising conceptions about the origin of prisons: The importance of economic considerations. *Social Science Quarterly, 62*, 249–257.

Conley, J. A. (1981). Prisons, production and profit: Reconsidering the importance of prison industries. *Journal of Social History, 53*, 259–275.

Ethridge, P. A. (1990). An analysis of the policy process pertaining to the utilization of private prisons in Texas. Unpublished doctoral dissertation, Sam Houston State University.

Folz, D. H., & Scheb, J. M. (1989). Prisons, profits, and politics: The Tennessee privatization. *Judicature, 73*, 98.

Gallagher, D., & Edwards, M. E. (1997). Prison industries and the private sector. *Atlantic Economic Journal, 25*, 91–98.

General Accounting Office (1997). *Private and public prisons: Studies comparing operational and/or quality of service* (U.S. GAO Letter Rep. GGD-96-158) [On-line]. Available: *http://www.securitymanagement.com:80/library /000231.html*.

Kingdon, J. (1984). *Agendas, alternatives and public policies*. Boston: Little, Brown.

Knepper, P. E. (1990). Imprisonment and society in Arizona territory. Unpublished doctoral dissertation, School of Justice Studies, Arizona State University.

Lanza-Kaduce, L., Parker, K. F., & Thomas, C. W. (1999). A comparative recidivism analysis of releases from private and public prisons. *Crime & Delinquency, 45*, 28–47.

Legislative Budget Committee for the State of Washington. (1996). *Department of Corrections privatization feasibility study*. Olympia, WA: Legislative Budget Committee.

Logan, C. H. (1990). *Private prisons: Pros and cons*. New York: Oxford University Press.

Logan, C. H. (1996). *Well kept: Comparing quality of confinement in a public and a private prison*. National Institute of Justice

Report [On-line]. Available: *http://www.uc.uconn.edu/-www-soci.*

Logan, C. H., & McGriff, B. (1989, September/October). *Comparing costs of public and private prisons. A case study* (National Institute of Justice Research in Brief Rep. No. 216). Washington, DC: National Institute of Justice

Maguire, K., & Pastore, A. L. (Eds.). (1994). *Sourcebook of criminal justice statistics.* Washington, DC: Bureau of Justice Statistics.

Maguire, K., & Pastore, A. L. (Eds.). (1996). *Sourcebook of criminal justice statistics.* Washington, DC: Bureau of Justice Statistics.

McDonald, D. C. (1990). The cost of operating public and private correctional facilities. In D. C. McDonald (Ed.), *Private prisons and the public interest* (pp. 86–106). New Brunswick, NJ: Rutgers University Press.

Prison Privatization Act, 128 Ariz. Rev. Stat. 41-1609, 1681-1684, 1803. (1997).

Schneider, A. (1998, September). Private prisons as public policy. Paper presented at the American Political Science Association Annual Conference, Boston.

Schneider, A., & Ingram, H. (1993). Social constructions and target populations: Implications for politics and policy. *American Political Science Review*, 87, 334–347.

Schneider, A., & Ingram, H. (1997). *Policy design for democracy.* Lawrence: University Press of Kansas.

Sechrest, D., & Shichor, D. (1993). Corrections goes public (and private) in California. *Federal Probation*, 57, 3–8.

Shichor, D. (1995). *Punishment for profit: Private prisons/public concerns.* Thousand Oaks: Sage.

Sparks, R. (1994). Can prisons be legitimate? Penal politics, privatization, and the timeliness of an old idea. *British Journal of Criminology*, 34, 14–28.

Tennessee Select Oversight Committee on Corrections. (1995). *Comparative evaluation of privately-managed CCA prison and state-managed prototypical prisons.* Nashville: Tennessee Legislature.

Texas Sunset Advisory Commission. (1991). Information report on contracts for correctional facilities and services. In *Recommendations to the Governor of Texas and members of the seventy-second legislature* (chap. 4). Austin, TX: Author.

Thomas, C. W. (1997). *Comparing the cost and performance of public and private prisons in Arizona.* Phoenix, AZ: Arizona Department of Corrections.

Thomas, C. W. (1998). *Evaluating the potential public policy implication of correctional privatization by the state of Iowa*. Miami: University of Florida.

Thomas, C. W. (1999). *Private prison project* [On-line]. Available: *http://web.crim.ufl.edu/pcp/census/*.

Thomas, C. W., Bolinger, D., & Badalamenti, J. L. (1997). *Private adult correctional facility census* (11th ed.). Private Corrections Project [On-line]. Available: *http:l/web.crim.ufl.edu/pcp/census/1997*.

Thomas, C. W., Bolinger, D., & Badalamenti, J. L. (1998). *Private adult correctional facility census* (11th ed.). Private Corrections Project [On-line]. Available: *http://web.crim.ufl.edu/pcp/census/1998*.

Walker, S. (1980). *Popular justice: A history of American criminal justice*. New York: Oxford University Press.

Private Prisons Not Saving Strapped Company Closing Three in Texas[2]

By Joseph T. Hallinan
TIMES-PICAYUNE, December 31, 1998

Come the first of the year, the nation's largest private prison company, the Corrections Corporation of America, will begin pulling up stakes in the country's largest private prison market, the state of Texas.

It will voluntarily quit running at least three prisons there, a small but telling omen in an industry grappling with change.

When private prisons first appeared in 1984, the companies that ran them promised big savings over government-run prisons.

But some of the savings aren't as big as officials had been led to believe. In some cases, the savings are less than 7 cents on the dollar.

This, along with other factors, has cooled privatization, one of the hottest trends in prisons. After years of breakneck growth, expansion is suddenly slowing and stock prices are flat or falling.

"You can't be a fledgling start-up forever," said Peggy Lawrence, vice president of investor relations for CCA, whose once-hot stock has taken a beating.

There are several reasons for the slowdown. Chief among them is fewer criminals. In December, the federal government announced that violent and property crimes hit their lowest level since 1973. And fewer crimes means fewer convicts.

"I guess the bottom line is, there's a bit of a slowdown in the number of inmates we've been receiving," said Larry Todd, a spokesman for the Texas Department of Criminal Justice.

Texas is the biggest private prison user in the country, swamping every other state. So a slowdown there has a disproportionate effect on the private prison industry.

Of the 142 private prisons and jails in operation in 1997, 41 of them—29 percent—were in Texas.

Fourteen of those were run by CCA until Dec. 31. But the company will stop running at least three of those jails, Lawrence said, as competition drives down the company's profits.

At the end of 1997, private prisons housed about 71,000 inmates, or about 4 percent of the nation's jail population.

These jails were built on a singular concept: Private is cheaper. But figuring out how much cheaper has been difficult. Industry estimates vary widely. CCA, which runs 72 prisons in the United States, cites savings ranging from 5 percent to 20 percent.

But the federal government, in a report released in 1996, said it could not conclude, based on the evidence, whether private prisons save any money at all.

The report, by the General Accounting Office, reviewed five separate studies that compared costs of public and private prisons.

In four of the comparisons examined, the GAO found that two showed no significant differences in cost, one showed a 7 percent difference in favor of the private prison, and another showed that the

---

But the federal government, in a report released in 1996, said it could not conclude, based on the evidence, whether private prisons save any money at all.

---

private prison was more expensive than one public prison but cheaper than another.

The fifth study reported that private prisons saved 14 percent to 15 percent. But the GAO discounted these results because the comparison was based on hypothetical public prisons, not real ones.

The state of Florida has also studied the issue, and has reached roughly the same conclusions as the GAO.

In a report released earlier this year, the state's equivalent of the GAO concluded that "private prisons are not providing the state with the level of overall costs savings initially projected."

The study, by the Office of Program Policy Analysis and Government Accountability, examined the first two private prisons built in Florida, one operated by CCA, the other by Wackenhut Corrections Corp. Both opened in 1995.

By law, private prisons in Florida must save at least 7 percent. But the Florida study found that both prisons fell short of this mark. The CCA prison provided no savings; Wackenhut's saved only 4 percent.

Both CCA and Wackenhut challenged the Florida study. John Rees, a CCA vice president, said in a letter that no prisons in Florida are comparable to the CCA facility. Therefore, he said, it was "impossible" and "reckless" to make comparisons.

John O'Rourke, Wackenhut's chief financial officer, said the state didn't properly credit Wackenhut's prison for certain income, including commissions earned from long-distance phone calls placed by inmates. If such credits had been made, he said, the company would have reached its 7 percent target.

Charles Thomas, a professor at the University of Florida and a leading expert on private prisons, has scaled back his growth forecasts for the industry, from 35 percent to 40 percent a year to a still-healthy 21 percent to 23 percent. Thomas is a member of the board of trustees of CCA Prison Realty Trust, a prison-owning company closely affiliated with CCA.

Between the end of 1997 and June 1999, Thomas predicts, 36 new prisons capable of holding nearly 30,000 inmates will have opened. This is a 13 percent drop from the 1996 pace.

The occupancy rate of private prisons is also slipping. According to numbers compiled by Thomas, private prisons filled 4 percent fewer beds in 1997 than in 1996.

Stock prices, too, are leveling off. The stock of CCA, which traded earlier this year for as much as $41.50, now languishes near $18.

Crime and Punishment[3]

By Cait Murphy
Fortune, April 30, 2001

Think that stuffing prisons with lawbreakers makes sense? You clearly haven't run the numbers. Here are some better ways to buy safety.

America is an exceptional country. Compared with citizens of other nations, Americans tend to be more religious and more entrepreneurial. We send more people to university, have more millionaires, and enjoy more living space. We are the world leaders in obesity and Nobel Prizes.

And we send people to prison at a rate that is almost unheard of. Right now, almost two million Americans are either in prison (after conviction) or jail (waiting for trial). Of every 100,000 Americans, 481 are in prison. By comparison, the incarceration rate for Britain is 125 per 100,000, for Canada 129, and for Japan 40. Only Russia, at 685, is quicker to lock 'em up.

America was not always so exceptional in this regard. For the 50 years prior to 1975, the U.S. incarceration rate averaged about 110, right around rich-world norms. But then, in the 1970s, the great prison buildup began. This was a bipartisan movement. Democrats like Jerry Brown of California and Ann Richards of Texas, for example, presided over prison population booms, as did Republican governors like John Ashcroft of Missouri and Michael Castle of Delaware. Bill Clinton worried in public about rising prison populations but signed legislation, much of it Republican sponsored, that kept the figures rising. No surprise, then, that spending on incarceration has ballooned from less than $7 billion in 1980 to about $45 billion today.

Just because the U.S. is different doesn't mean it is wrong. But prison is a serious matter in a way that, say, America's inexplicable affection for tractor pulls is not. Accordingly, a number of people— social scientists, prison professionals, even a few politicians—have begun to examine how and why the U.S. sends people to prison. What they are finding, in broad terms, is that there is a substantial minority of prisoners for whom incarceration is inappropriate—and much too expensive.

---

3. Article by Cait Murphy from *Fortune* April 30, 2001. Copyright © 2001 Time Inc. All rights reserved.

Who deserves to be imprisoned is, of course, partly a question of moral values. Prison keeps criminals off the streets; it punishes transgressors and deters people from committing crimes. But it is also a question of economic values. Everyone agrees that caging, say, John Wayne Gacy is worth whatever it costs, but that locking up a granny caught shoplifting makes no sense. The question to consider, then, is not "Does prison work?" but "*When* does prison work?" Economics can help draw the line.

On one level, it makes sense that America imprisons more people than its peers. The U.S. has historically been more violent than Europe, Japan, or Canada—in particular, our homicide rate is well above

> *The question to consider, then, is not "Does prison work?" but "When does prison work?" Economics can help draw the line.*

world norms—and the public wants violent people punished while freeing society from their presence. "We are a culture that believes change is possible, that human beings can be saved," says Francis Cullen of the University of Cincinnati, who specializes in public attitudes toward crime and rehabilitation. "The dividing line is violence. That's where people start becoming unwilling to take risks." Fundamentally, America's prison population grew because people got sick of feeling scared and elected politicians who promised to deliver freedom from that fear. Moreover, it could be argued that America had some catching up to do: From the early 1960s to the early 1970s, the violent-crime rate rose sharply while the incarceration rate actually fell. Those trends probably helped spawn the "tough on crime" mentality that has reigned since. In the 1980s lawmakers delivered mandatory minimums—statutory requirements for harsh sentences for certain offenses, mostly gun-and-drug-related. In the 1990s came "three-strikes" laws, designed to target repeat felons; truth-in-sentencing legislation; and the abolition of parole in many states.

All those policies filled prisons, but not necessarily with the hardened thugs people thought they were putting away. Though there are now 400,000 more violent offenders behind bars than there were in 1980, the proportion of violent offenders in the prison population has actually fallen. According to the Bureau of Justice Statistics, the percentage of violent offenders in state prisons has dropped from almost 60% in 1980 to 48% at the end of 1999; 21% were in prison in 1999 for property crimes, 21% for drug crimes, and the rest for public-order offenses, such as immigration, vice, or weapons violations. In the federal system, home to about 145,000 offenders, 58% are in for drug offenses (compared with 25% in 1980) and only 12%

for violent crimes—down from 17% in 1990. Of the six crimes that account for the great majority of prisoners (murder, robbery, aggravated assault, burglary, drugs, and sexual assault), drug offenders made up 45% of the growth from 1980 to 1996, figures Allan Beck of the BJS. Every year from 1990 through 1997, more people were sentenced to prison for drug offenses than for violent crimes.

Because imprisonment went up in the 1990s and crime went down, you might conclude that locking up so many criminals bought us less crime. Up to a point that's true. Steven Levitt, a professor of economics at the University of Chicago, has cleverly provided an empirical foundation to prove the link between incarceration and crime reduction. In 1996 he studied what happened after the courts ordered 12 states to reduce overcrowding in their prison systems. By looking at how the states responded, either by releasing convicts or by building new prisons, he estimated that the effect of imprisoning one additional lawbreaker for a year was to prevent two fewer violent crimes and about a dozen fewer property crimes. The social costs of these crimes Levitt estimated at $53,900 (a figure derived from published estimates commonly used by social scientists). That's well above the $25,000 or so it costs to keep a prisoner behind bars for a year.

> *As more and more people are imprisoned, the nastiness of the inmate population diminishes, so the crime control delivered per convict drops.*

But that doesn't prove that every prison cell built in America's 25-year construction spree was worth it. There could be ways to deliver just as much public safety for less money. Take Canada. Like the U.S., Canada saw a sharp decline in violent crime in the 1990s—but while America's prison population almost doubled, Canada's rose only slightly. Or take next-door neighbors New Hampshire and Maine. In the first half of the 1990s, both saw similar declines in crime, but New Hampshire sharply increased the number of people it imprisoned, while Maine did not. Ditto for Kansas and Missouri; the latter built lots more new prisons, but the crime rates in the two states remained similar. In short, building prisons is not the only way to fight crime—and often not a cost-effective way to do so.

In economic terms, this is because not every prison cell delivers equal returns, in terms of havoc unwreaked. As more and more people are imprisoned, the nastiness of the inmate population diminishes, so the crime control delivered per convict drops. Consider the research of John DiIulio, the new director of President Bush's office of faith-based programs; Bert Useem, director of the Institute for Social Research at the University of New Mexico; and Anne Morrison Piehl, a professor of public policy at Harvard's Kennedy School of Government. In 1999 the trio surveyed male inmates in Arizona,

New Mexico, and New York about their criminal pasts. Then they multiplied each crime by its social cost, using National Institute of Justice numbers. (The cost of a rape, for example, is estimated at $98,327; of a burglary, $1,271.)

They found that the social cost of the crimes committed by the median inmate in New York—that is, one whose crimes rank 50 on a scale of 100 in terms of seriousness—was $31,866; in New Mexico, $26,486; and in Arizona, $25,472. That's slightly more than the $25,000 cost of incarceration. For the 40th percentile, though, that figure dropped to less than $14,000 in all three states, and for the 20th, less than $7,000. At the 80th percentile, the monetary value of crime caused was almost $240,000 for New York and $163,311 for New Mexico—marking the perpetrator as the type of person for whom prison is clearly an appropriate solution.

On the subject of drug treatment, cost-benefit analysis has something to say: It works.

The major dividing line between cost-effective and non-cost-effective incarceration? That turns out to be fairly easy to figure. As a general rule, those who were imprisoned for property or violent crimes caused damage to society that cost more than their incarceration; those convicted solely of drug offenses did not.

Drug dealing is not harmless, of course. Having an open-air crack market on the corner kills commerce and devastates neighborhoods. But the authors became convinced that the incarceration of so many drug-only offenders—28% in New York and 18% in Arizona—made no economic sense, because one drug seller sent to prison just created a job opening for another seller. Consider the example of a Milwaukee street corner. In 1996 a Wisconsin task force noted that although the police had made 94 drug-related arrests in three months at the corner of 9th and Concordia, most of them leading to prison sentences, the drug market continued and public safety did not improve. And the price was substantial: It costs about $23 million to jail 94 people for a year.

In short, the authors found that for drug offenders, "the crime averted by incarceration is low," says Piehl. "We need to come up with sanctions that are graduated so that our only options are not nothing, or prison, or probation." What made that conclusion particularly noteworthy was that Piehl and DiIulio had argued for years in favor of more prisons. But by last year DiIulio, who is no one's idea of a bleeding-heart liberal, was writing an article for the editorial page of the *Wall Street Journal* titled "Two Million Prisoners Is Enough."

Are there better, less costly alternatives to prison for drug offenders? Lisa Roberson offers one answer to that question. She is a resident at the Phoenix Career Academy in Brooklyn, N.Y., which offers residents—many of them repeat offenders who would otherwise be in prison—intensive drug treatment, vocational training, and after-care assistance. Roberson, 31, who started selling drugs at 17 and using them at 21, spent four years at Clinton State in New Jersey for selling drugs to an undercover cop. "All I did there is learn how to jail," she says. When she was arrested again in 2000, the court gave her a choice: prison or two years at Phoenix.

This is no country club. Residents sleep ten to a room. Just about every minute of their day, starting with a 6 A.M. wake-up call, is plotted for them. If Roberson makes it through the program—and about 60% do—she will be drug-free and will have completed training as a drug counselor. Phoenix will help her find a job, an apartment, and child care for her 4-year-old son. Yes, Roberson may regress—of those who complete the course, about a third eventually go back to drugs—but clearly she has a much better shot at establishing a real life than if she had spent several more years "learning how to jail." The cost of her treatment, funded mostly by state and local governments: $17,000 to $18,000 a year.

Many successful drug-treatment programs are run out of prisons too—such as Amity Righturn, a program in a medium-security facility in San Diego that provides more than a year of assessment and counseling, plus further treatment after the inmates have left prison. A 1999 study found that three years after release, 27% of inmates who completed all three parts of the program had returned to prison; among those who got no treatment, 75% did.

On the subject of drug treatment, cost-benefit analysis has something to say: It works. Numerous studies have concluded that well-run drug-treatment programs, particularly long-term residential ones with follow-up care, can pay for themselves just by reducing crime. Add in the value of incarceration avoided and taxes paid by the freed, and it adds up.

Given this context, it's little short of tragic that drug-treatment programs in prison are not keeping pace with the need for them. In 1991 about a third of the inmates who reported drug use in the month prior to their arrest were getting treatment; by 1999 that was down to less than 15%, according to the Department of Justice, and much of that was of the nonintensive variety that has little long-term effect. Treatment is no panacea: Lots of people will drop out or go back to their bad habits. The point is simply that treatment works often enough for the benefits to outweigh the costs—the exact opposite of the economics of prison for drug offenders.

What about other prison programs? Social scientists have applied cost-benefit analysis to those too. They have found that busy inmates—those given the chance to learn to read, to finish high school, to learn basic job skills—are significantly less likely than idle ones to return to prison. In Maryland, for example, a follow-up analysis published last October of 1,000 former inmates found a 19% lower recidivism rate for those who had taken education programs in prison than for those who hadn't. Extrapolating that 19% figure for the state as a whole suggests that Maryland could save $23.2 million a year in reduced incarceration—double what it spends on prison education programs.

More evidence that educational programs save money: In 1999 analysts from the state of Washington surveyed studies dating back to the mid-1970s on what works and what fails in reducing crime. The researchers concluded that for every dollar spent on basic adult education in prison, there was $1.71 in reduced crime; for every dollar on vocational education, $3.23.

If you think such data have prompted more educational programs in prisons, think again. Congress passed "get tough" legislation in the 1990s that eliminated Pell grants to prisoners for college courses; it also reduced the requirements for basic and vocational education for prisoners. Many states have therefore taken the opportunity to cut back. Prisoners have a limited constituency, after all, and nixing programs for them is a politically painless way to cut budgets.

Ironically, surveys show that the public strongly supports prisoner-rehabilitation programs. So do many who run the prisons. Tommy Douberley, warden of Florida's Moore Haven Correctional

Table 1: Incarceration Rate per 100,000 residents

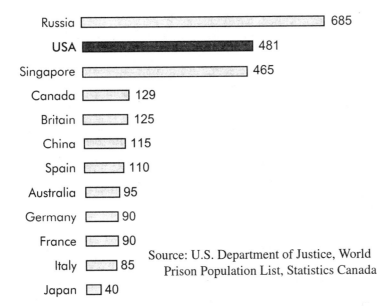

Country	Rate
Russia	685
USA	481
Singapore	465
Canada	129
Britain	125
China	115
Spain	110
Australia	95
Germany	90
France	90
Italy	85
Japan	40

Source: U.S. Department of Justice, World Prison Population List, Statistics Canada

Table 2: U.S. Prison Population*

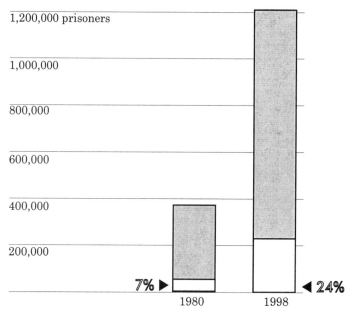

* In state and federal prisons. Does not include the 76,000
people in private prisons, or those in jail awaiting trial.

Facility, is convinced that no-frills prisons are a mistake. "These
people are going to be returned to society," he says. "We need to
make some provision for them that when they get out they are better than when they went in." Politicians, however, seem to have
interpreted the public's clear desire for greater safety as a mandate
for more and harsher prisons. And they are not the same thing at
all.

There are signs that America is beginning to recognize the limits
of prison. Drug offenders are less likely to be sentenced to prison
today than they were in 1992 (though still more than three times as
likely as in 1980), in part because of the emergence of drug courts in
many states, which force defendants into treatment on pain of
prison. But past policies continue to exert expansionary pressure.
From June 1999 to June 2000, the last 12-month period for which
figures are available, the incarcerated population rose 3%. Though
the smallest rise in decades, that still meant that 31,000 more
Americans were behind bars. To house them means building a
prison every ten days or so—an expensive hobby, considering that a
medium-security facility for 1,000 inmates can cost $50 million.

Make no mistake: A large proportion of inmates thoroughly
deserve to be exactly where they are. Incarceration is an effective
way to isolate really awful people. But too many prisons stuffed

with nonviolent, idle inmates is simply wasteful, of both people and money. We would do better to learn from several states that have lowered the crime rate without substantially raising prison populations—as New York did at least in part by aggressively funneling drug offenders into treatment, for example. Instead of being exceptional for its willingness to jail its citizens, the goal for America should be to become exceptional in the application of wisdom to its criminal population. At the moment, it is not even close.

IV. Unequal Representation: Minorities and Women in Prison

Editor's Introduction

In the U.S. almost one-third of all African-American men between the ages of 20 and 29 are under the control of a correctional institution. Between 1985 and 1995 the rate of incarceration of African-American men grew from 3,544 per 100,000 to 6,926 per 100,000. For whites during this period, the rates increased from 528 per 100,000 to 919 per 100,000, whereas the incarceration rate of Hispanics was somewhere between that for African-Americans and whites. What are the reasons for this disparity? There is no consensus on the issue. Some argue that police target poor urban neighborhoods, many of which are dominated by racial minorities. Some claim that our courts discriminate against racial minorities, dispensing more convictions and longer sentences to these groups. Some say minorities simply commit more crimes. All agree, however, that the racial disparity in our prisons is closely related to drugs, since most people convicted of drug-related crimes are minorities.

Racial discrepancies also exist in the female inmate population. Approximately one million women are now overseen by the U.S. correctional system. As of 1998 women accounted for 6.5 percent of the state prison population, up from 4.1 percent in 1980. Because the numbers of women arrested increased by 24 percent in the 1990s (as opposed to the 13 percent increase for men), women will likely comprise an even greater percentage of prisoners in the future.

Section IV begins with two articles about race in prisons and concludes with two articles about female inmates. In "Report: War on Drugs Sends Blacks to Prisons at 13 Times Rate of Whites," Michael A. Fletcher highlights a 2000 study by the Human Rights Watch which shows that 482 of every 100,000 African-American men are imprisoned for drug-related crimes, compared to 36 of every 100,000 white men. The report, Fletcher notes, coincides with a number of studies that show similar statistics.

Jesse Katz, in "Voting Rights for Felons Debated," explains that, due to the large number of African-American men in prison and the voting restrictions for prisoners, at any given time one in seven African-American males cannot vote. In most states the right to vote is regained upon the serving of one's full sentence, but in 12 states the right is permanently revoked.

In "Tougher Sentencing, Economic Hardships, and Rising Violence," Leonard Curry chronicles the growing rate of female incarceration in the U.S. and examines the role of drug offenses in this increase. He documents the proliferation of imprisoned mothers, as well as the increase in the incidence of HIV/AIDS among female inmates.

Observing specific cases of the same trend reported by Curry, Ron Stodghill II, in "Unequal Justice: Why Women Fare Worse," connects the rise of mandatory-minimum sentencing to the growing number of women serving prison terms for first-time drug offenses. He tells the story of Kellie Ann Mann and others whose husbands or boyfriends deal drugs. These women, peripherally connected to the crimes, served or are serving long prison terms partly because they did not know enough to provide information for plea bargains.

War on Drugs Sends Blacks to Prison at 13 Times Rate of Whites[1]

By Michael A. Fletcher
Washington Post, June 8, 2000

The nation's war on drugs unfairly targets African-Americans, who are far more likely to be imprisoned for drug offenses than whites, even though far more whites use illegal drugs than blacks, according to a new report by the advocacy group Human Rights Watch.

The report, to be released today, said that African-Americans accounted for 62 percent of the drug offenders sent to state prisons nationwide in 1996, the most recent year for which statistics are available, although they represent just 12 percent of the U.S. population. Overall, black men are sent to state prisons on drug charges at 13 times the rate of white men, according to the study, which analyzes a wide range of Justice Department information for 37 states to come up with its findings.

These disparities exist even though data gathered by the Department of Health and Human Services show that in 1991, 1992 and 1993, about five times as many whites had used cocaine than blacks, the report said. The report added that drug transactions among blacks often are easier for police to target because they more often occur in public than do drug transactions among whites.

"These racial disparities are a national scandal," said Ken Roth, executive director of Human Rights Watch, an international human rights organization. "Black and white drug offenders get radically different treatment in the American justice system. This is not only profoundly unfair to blacks, it also corrodes the American ideal of equal justice for all."

The disparities are particularly striking in individual states, where black men are sent to prison on drug charges at rates as much as 57 times greater than that of white men. In Maryland, for example, blacks make up 27 percent of the population and 90 percent of those sent to prison on drug charges—for a rate that is 28 times greater than whites.

In Virginia, meanwhile, blacks are 82 percent of those sent to prison on drug charges and just 20 percent of the population. Overall, they are sent to prison on drug charges at a rate 21 times greater than whites.

"More blacks were sent to state prison nationwide on drug charges than for crimes of violence," Jamie Fellner, associate counsel for Human Rights Watch, wrote in the report. "Only 27 percent of black admissions to prison were for crimes of violence—compared to 38 percent for drug offenses."

The Human Rights Watch report adds to a growing array of studies documenting racial disparities in the nation's criminal justice system. A report last month by the Leadership Conference on Civil Rights found that African-Americans and Hispanics are treated more harshly than similarly situated whites at every level of the criminal justice system. And that report came on the heels of a study by the National Council on Crime and Delinquency showing that black and Hispanic youth are more likely than whites to be arrested, prosecuted, held in jail without bail and sentenced to long prison terms.

Remedies suggested in the Human Rights Watch report include the repeal of mandatory sentencing laws for drug offenders, increasing drug treatment and eliminating racial profiling as a police tactic.

Largely because of the huge disparity in imprisonment for drug offenses, blacks are sent to prison at 8.2 times the rate of whites. Overall, one in 20 black men over the age of 18 is in a state or federal prison, compared to one in 180 white men.

"Prison is a legitimate criminal sanction," the report said. "But it should be used sensibly, justly, parsimoniously, and with due consideration . . . and respect for human dignity required by international human rights law. The incarceration of hundreds of thousands of low-level, non-violent drug offenders betrays indifference to such considerations."

Voting Rights for Felons Debated[2]

BY JESSE KATZ
DETROIT NEWS, APRIL 28, 2000

The assignment was one of the biggest of J. C. Towns' photographic career: Snap the official campaign portrait of Eastside Selma's leading politician, a man vying to become the city's first black mayor.

For several weeks now, Towns' picture of the candidate has been plastered on billboards across this fabled Southern community, hallowed ground in the struggle for black voting rights. But when the candidate asked Towns for his vote—black turnout being the key to toppling the nine-term incumbent—the founder of New Life Photo Ministries had to shake his head.

"I'm a criminal, man, a convict, a stain on society," said Towns, 50. Nineteen years ago, he explained, he was found guilty of possessing stolen property, an offense that disqualifies him from voting in Alabama despite having served four years in prison and two on parole.

"I'm not a trouble person," Towns said, "but I ain't got no rights."

As the nation heads to the polls this year, a large and growing segment of the population is being excluded from the practice of democracy: Nearly 4 million felons—some incarcerated, others long since free—are without the right to vote. In most states, that right is automatically restored after a convict completes his sentence or the terms of his parole. But in 12 states, convicts lose their voting rights indefinitely, leaving at least 1.7 million adults disenfranchised for life, according to estimates by the Sentencing Project, a liberal think tank in Washington that studies the social costs of the United States' prison boom.

Black men, disproportionately represented in the criminal justice system to begin with, bear the brunt of these laws: At any given time, one in seven cannot vote. In the states that continue to penalize felons after their sentences have been served, the rate is closer to one in four. In Alabama, the nation's disenfranchisement leader, roughly one in three black men is stripped of his vote—a penalty that, to many here, echoes the Jim Crow tactics that once kept nearly all blacks from being counted.

"This is the modern-day version of the poll tax and the literacy test," said J. L. Chestnut Jr., Selma's first black lawyer.

---

2. Article by Jesse Katz from *Detroit News* April 28, 2000. Copyright © Los Angeles Times Syndicate. Reprinted with permission.

People who favor disenfranchisement say that the felon has only himself to blame. States deny ex-cons all kinds of privileges—owning a gun, obtaining an occupational license, serving on a jury—based on the rationale that society has the prerogative, even the duty, to restrict the civic participation of any citizen who acts against the common good.

"I don't care if they're Hispanic, black, white or whatever—I just take a dim view of anyone who breaks the law," said Alabama state Rep. Bob McKee, a leading Republican from Montgomery.

The practice dates back centuries to ancient Rome and, later, medieval Europe, where infamous criminals would be sentenced to "civil death," banished from the communities they victimized. "It can scarcely be deemed unreasonable," 2nd U.S. Circuit Court of Appeals Judge Henry J. Friendly once ruled, "for a state to decide that perpetrators of serious crimes shall not take part in electing

---

Each state determines voter eligibility, even for presidential races, allowing a rapist in Illinois to help pick the nation's next leader but not a bad-check writer in Mississippi.

---

the legislators who make the laws, the executives who enforce these, the prosecutors who must try them for further violations, or the judges who are to consider their cases."

To critics, disenfranchisement is an undemocratic relic, left over from a time when only white, landowning men had access to the ballot. The redeeming feature of American political history, as they see it, has been the steady expansion of suffrage: to the poor, women, racial minorities, young adults.

Few people go so far as to urge that felons be permitted to cast a ballot behind bars—a privilage granted by only three, Maine, Massachusetts and Vermont. But many consider permanent punishment to be cruel and self-defeating, a stigma that undermines the offender's already tenuous place in society. "Politics is all a bunch of baloney," said John Casby, an ex-con who lives in a blistered shotgun shack not far from the Alabama Capitol. "But it's still all right, you know what I mean? Everyone wants to be recognized."

A retired cashier at the Gunter Air Force Base commissary in Montgomery, Casby lost his voting rights 25 years ago after shooting a woman in the shoulder during a whiskey-sopped fight over money. He spent 21 days in jail, served 10 years' probation and—using the settlement from an auto accident—eventually handed over $10,000 in restitution.

"It might've been different if I'd have killed her," he said. "But I did my time, and I paid my debt. Now I want to be a citizen again."

Congress is considering a bill—the Civic Participation and Rehabilitation Act—that would extend voting rights to probationers, parolees and ex-cons in federal elections. As it stands now, each state determines voter eligibility, even for presidential races, allowing a rapist in Illinois to help pick the nation's next leader but not a bad-check writer in Mississippi.

Such a crazy quilt of rules might appear intrinsically unfair, reducing voting rights to an accident of geography. But many legal scholars believe Congress has no authority to meddle; the Constitution's 14th Amendment, which imposes penalties on states that fail to provide equal access to the ballot, specifically exempts cases of disenfranchisement due to "rebellion, or other crime."

"We do not want people voting who are not trustworthy and loyal to our republic," Roger Clegg, a former deputy in the Justice Department's civil rights division under the Bush administration, told the House Judiciary Committee last fall. He added: "Criminals are, in the aggregate, less likely to be trustworthy good citizens."

How crimes are defined, enforced, prosecuted and sentenced is a matter of intense debate in this country. As the U.S. jail and prison population swells—doubling from 1 million to 2 million in the last decade—so does the racial disparity; blacks are seven times more likely than whites to end up behind bars.

In the South, moreover, laws historically have been tailored in ways that have made blacks more susceptible to arrest.

"There have always been mechanisms for diluting, or destroying, the black vote," said Slema lawyer J.L. Chestnut, who helped carry the Rev. Maring Luther King's injured marchers to safety after state troopers, on "Bloody Sunday," violently blocked them from crossing the Edmund Pettus Bridge. "After the civil rights movement, that mechanism became the criminal justice system—and here in Alabama, they have used it to the hilt."

To the defenders of disenfranchisement, any effort to deflect blame from the criminal serves only to demean those who choose not to break the law. They contend that blacks—who are more likely than whites to live in high-crime areas—have the greatest interest in keeping political power out of the hands of their victimizers.

Tougher Sentencing, Economic Hardships and Rising Violence[3]

By Leonard Curry
Corrections Today, February 2001

There has been a shift in the gender composition of the nation's correctional population, for more than 950,000 females are under correctional supervision. This shift has been caused by tougher substance abuse sentencing guidelines, economic hardships and rising violence levels among women. Although the male inmate population remains significantly larger, the escalating numbers of women in prison are causing a tilt in the U.S. prison population.

An Increasing Trend

Within the past 20 years, statistics show that there has been an increasing trend in the amount of women being arrested, incarcerated and placed under supervision. These statistics indicate that the numbers are continuing to increase and also show that these women have come from similar backgrounds and have common characteristics.

In 1998, women accounted for 6.5 percent of state prison populations an increase from the 1980 statistic of 4.1 percent, according to the Bureau of Justice Statistics (BJS). This trend is expected to continue because arrests of women have been rising at a faster rate than men—a 24 percent increase in the early 1990s, compared to a 13 percent increase for males. In 1998, women accounted for more than one out of five of the nation's 14.4 million arrests.

The average increase in female incarceration in the 1990s was 8.3 percent and the annual rate of women sentenced to jails and prisons exceeded 10 percent in 18 states, led by Tennessee at 15 percent, North Dakota at 14.9 percent, Montana at 14.7 and Idaho at 14.3 percent.

According to BJS, most incarcerated females have monthly incomes of less than $600 at the time of arrest, have suffered physical or sexual abuse, and have grown up in single parent households.

---

3. Reprinted with persioon of the American Correctional Association, Lanham, Md.

Drug Offenses

The 1990s have shown a significant increase in the amount of women being charged for drug and alcohol use as well as an increase in incarcerated repeat drug offenders. Although most sentences can be traced to substance abuse, violent crime also is on the rise.

Of the women in all prisons and jails, 34 percent are serving time for drug offenses and 32 percent for property offenses often related to crimes committed to support drug habits. By self-admission, three of every four are substance abusers. At the federal level, 72 percent of female inmates were sentenced for drug offenses.

The population of females incarcerated for more than one year soared 79 percent in the 1990s, primarily due to new sentencing guidelines that required incarceration for repeat drug offenders, according to BJS. Prison sentences for most women can be traced to

---

Of the women in all prisons and jails, 34 percent are serving time for drug offenses and 32 percent for property offenses often related to crimes committed to support drug habits.

---

substance abuse, however, there has been a significant rise in both violent crime and recidivism.

BJS reported that the number of state and federal female inmates more than doubled from 44,065 in 1990 to 90,668 in 1999. "Women were being charged in the 1990s for offenses that they were not charged with in earlier years—drug and alcohol use," said a BJS statistician. "Most of the women are from lower socioeconomic backgrounds and they buy their drugs on the street, while women from middle and upper-income brackets get prescriptions or buy from dealers who are not standing on street corners," the statistician said.

In addition, the General Accounting Office found that the number of women incarcerated for drug offenses nearly doubled from 1990 to 1997. Black women are more than twice as likely as Hispanic women and eight times as likely as white women to be incarcerated for drug offenses.

Regional Increases

The largest increments of the female inmate population were in the South and the West, which doubled over the decade. According to BJS, the female population in Southern prisons soared 144 percent (37,525), while Western female prison populations grew 96 percent (19,333). California had the second largest number of women in prison—11,368. Of the 22,159 rise in the South, Texas accounted for nearly half (10,306 inmates) a more than 400 percent increase from 2,196 in 1990 to 12,502 in 1999. Female inmates jumped 88 percent (14,143) in Midwest states and increased 55 percent to 9,754 in the Northeast.

BJS statistics also show that among the large states, New York showed the smallest change, but still grew 35 percent. Vermont's female inmates declined from 24 in 1991 to 22 in 1998. The other states with fewer than 100 imprisoned females were Maine, North Dakota and Rhode Island.

Incarcerated Mothers

The number of children with incarcerated parents rose 60 percent in the 1990s and by 1999, affected one of every 50 children. The prison population grew at nearly that time pace 62 percent—during that period, reports BJS. Fewer than half the children were living with parents before incarceration and fewer than half visited the incarcerated parents. However, about 60 percent of inmate mothers reported either getting telephone calls or mail from their children each week. Incarcerated Parents and Their Children, a BJS report, found that nearly 1.5 million minor children have mothers or fathers in prison, an increase of more than 500,000 since 1991.

Of the nation's 72 million minor children (up to age 17), an estimated 2 percent had imprisoned parents in 1999. In 1999, 721,500 federal and state inmates had minor children. More than half the children with incarcerated parents (58 percent) were younger than 10—the average age was 8.

Incarcerated parents were overwhelmingly male (93 percent) and predominantly held in state prisons, rather than federal facilities (89 percent compared to 11 percent). The number of incarcerated women with minor children rose 98 percent to 126,100 betweeen 1991 and 1999.

Half the parents in state prisons were black, about one-quarter were white and one-fifth were Hispanic. In 1999, an estimated 767,200 black children, 384,500 white children and 301,600 Hispanic children had parents in prison. The percentage of black children with incarcerated parents (7 percent) was nearly nine times higher than that of white children (0.8 percent). Hispanic children were three times as likely as white children to have parents in prison (2.6 percent).

State inmate parents were less likely to be violent offenders (44 percent) than inmates without children (51 percent). Three-quarters of state inmates who were parents had prior convictions, and the majority (56 percent) had previously been incarcerated.

About 60 percent of parents in state prisons reported having used drugs in the month before their offenses and 25 percent reported histories of alcohol dependence. More than one-third of parents committed their offenses while under the influence of alcohol. About 14 percent of parents reported mental illnesses; 70 percent of parents did not have high school diplomas; and 27 percent of parents were unemployed at the time of their arrests.

Women's Health Care in Prison

Pregnancy, drug and alcohol addiction, HIV/AIDS and other sexually transmitted diseases (STDs) are just a few factors that make women's health care in prison a unique challenge. These problems are on the rise as the female prison population increases. Although data show that these women have a greater need for health care, health care distribution has been unbalanced, particularly in smaller states.

Even in the largest jurisdictions California, Texas and the federal system—which house one-third of the female inmates, health care is disproportionate. Civil rights attorneys brought lawsuits against the Central California Women's Facility in Chowchilla and the California Institution for Women in Frontera to improve the delivery of health care, although the circumstances were extreme because a contract laboratory in 1997 falsified the results of Pap smears and hepatitis and HIV tests.

Conclusion

The incidence of HIV among women inmates is 50 percent higher than among males and the prevalence of mental illness is more than twice as high among women than men. One in every 20 female inmates is pregnant at admission.

Drug and alcohol use, unemployment, a history of sexual abuse and incomplete education are several factors that contribute to the increasing trend of women in prison. Although the male inmate population remains significantly larger, the female prison population has been escalating at a high rate during the past several years. The amont of women with HIV, AIDS and other STDs also has increased, causing unique challenges in the prison health care system. Pregnancy and incarcerated mothers also have caused a challenge for the prison system. The larger the increase, the larger these challenges will be in the coming years.

Unequal Justice: Why Women Fare Worse[4]

By Ron Stodghill II
TIME, February 1, 1999

It can be said now, perhaps, that Kellie Ann Mann's first crime was falling in love with a guy like Patrick. Before she met the popular, streetwise boy whose curly, shoulder-length blond hair and swaggering gait sent girls' hearts racing, Mann was just another middle-class Atlanta teenager crossing the rocky terrain of adolescence. Once, twice at most, she toked a joint. Then, she says, one night in 1986, outside Crestwood High School in Roswell, Ga., with Patrick sitting beside her in her new silver Volkswagen Golf, she took her first hit of LSD. "My parents were divorcing, and I guess I was rebelling," says Mann, who was 16 at the time. "Besides, I thought Patrick was all of the things I wanted to be."

As it turned out, Patrick in time came under drug surveillance by federal agents. Mann claims she knew only of Patrick's penchant for using drugs, not selling them. Under Patrick's tutelage, she says, she experimented with acid, cocaine, even heroin, and took to the road for stoned-out trips to Grateful Dead concerts.

But parties, no matter how spirited, always come to an end, and by 1992, Mann had quit both drugs and Patrick and plunged into her studies in anthropology at a college in Santa Rosa, Calif. Mann says it was during this sober period that, as one last favor to her old sweetheart, she made a mistake she will forever regret. She mailed Patrick 30 sheets of LSD that she had bought from a local dealer. "I know people think, 'Here's this middle-class white girl who had everything going for her, and she screwed it up.' But I was 21. I was a kid, and I made a poor choice."

Today Mann, 28, is an inmate serving 10 years at Alderson Federal Prison Camp, a minimum-security facility tucked away in the foothills of the Allegheny Mountains in West Virginia. Her story is common among the institution's nearly 800 women prisoners. "It's fairly simple," says Richard Russell, executive assistant at Alderson. "A lot of women here got sucked in with a boyfriend involved in drugs." More than 70% of the inmates at Alderson are, like Mann, first-time offenders convicted of nonviolent, drug-related crimes serving sentences ranging, in most cases, from 12 months to 14 years.

In the ruckus over mandatory-minimum-sentencing laws, the sharp impact on first-time women offenders is stirring considerable debate. Since 1980 the number of women in state and federal prisons has tripled, to 78,000, according to the Bureau of Justice Statistics. A major reason is that women, generally small players in drug trafficking, don't possess enough information about the operation to plea-bargain sentence reductions. In many cases they simply refuse to snitch on loved ones and family members or to cooperate by wearing wiretaps or going undercover.

> *Women drug offenders often wind up with a longer prison sentence than the drug-dealing men they're involved with.*

The result is that women drug offenders often wind up with a longer prison sentence than the drug-dealing men they're involved with. In Mann's case, former boyfriend Patrick provided details on various suspected drug dealers and walked free after serving 34 months. (Patrick could not be reached for comment.) "It's unfortunate, but most times women just don't know enough to be helpful and trade information," says Mark Mauer, assistant director of the U.S. Sentencing Project. Monica Pratt, a spokeswoman for the Families Against Mandatory Minimums Foundation, puts it this way: "It's America's dirty secret that in so many drug cases the least culpable gets left holding the bag."

To be sure, it's tough to find a criminal—or an advocate for one—who believes his or her punishment fits the crime. And the rippling social consequences of selling drugs in large quantities are so enormous, in both human and monetary terms, that dealers shouldn't go unpunished. But in case after case at Alderson, women appear to have been scapegoats and gofers in the operation rather than the kingpins the law was created to nab. "Nobody should get off scot-free for selling drugs," says Kathy Nelson, 36, a first-time offender and mother of two children, who is serving 10 years at Alderson for helping her husband distribute cocaine and marijuana. "I'm just saying when they're putting up women's prisons faster than Wal-Marts, then we've got a problem."

Before the mandatory-minimum-sentencing laws, judges could use their discretion in considering all the mitigating circumstances of a case. Now, though, first-time offenders like Joanne Tucker, 47, have little chance of getting a break in court. Tucker's troubles began back in 1987, when she was working as a customer-service representative for an insurance agency in Atlanta and her husband Gary opened a garden store selling hydroponic gear for growing plants indoors without soil. Tucker claims she was never involved in the business except for some occasional bookkeeping. That didn't matter to DEA agents. Suspecting that customers were growing cannabis with merchandise purchased at the store, they began trailing the customers home and raiding their houses. Many of those charged with manufacturing marijuana reduced their sentences by testifying that both Joanne and Gary gave them advice on how to grow the drug.

As she sits wearing her khaki prison uniform, Joanne, serving a 10-year sentence along with Gary for conspiracy to manufacture marijuana, insists that she committed no crime and was unaware of any illegal activities. "I don't feel guilty or ashamed about being here because I didn't do anything wrong," she claims. "If Gary knew anything, he never told me about it." Then, bitterly, she adds, "When you're the wife, you're always the last to know."

V. Behind the Bars:
Prison Conditions

Editor's Introduction

I n February 2000 officials of the state of Michigan announced that a number of its prisoners who had been housed in Virginia prisons were coming home. Since 1998 Michigan had sent about 2,500 inmates to Virginia due to overcrowding in its own prisons, but reductions in its prison population allowed the state to take back its prisoners. This was indicative of general trends across the nation, as prison construction and the decelerating incarceration rate reduced the average prison capacity from 115% in 1990 to 109% in 1999. Nevertheless, overcrowding is still a problem in many states, and the related problems of violence and poor health conditions persist.

In New York, for instance, approximately 6,000 to 7,000 of the 70,000 prisoners suffer from HIV, which can lead to AIDS, and 20 percent of the prisoners have Hepatitis C. The percentage is even higher in Texas and California, the latter of which recently came under fire from inmates filing lawsuits to protest inadequate healthcare in state prisons.

Furthermore, violence is prevalent in many prisons, causing dangerous situations for inmates and guards. Gangs, often aligned along racial lines, rule prisons, forcing newcomers to join in order to protect themselves. In "Prisoner's Dilemma" Michael Berryhill reflects upon the murder of James Byrd Jr., an African-American man who was brutally murdered by three white men, two of whom—John William King and Lawrence Russell Brewer—had served time in Texas prisons. As shocking as Byrd's death was, Berryhill argues, it was not unique. "King and Brewer have opened a window onto what happens on a frequent basis in Texas's vast prison system," writes Berryhill.

Prison administrators have, of course, attempted to reduce violence in their prisons, and the final two articles in this section look at the security measures that many new medium- and high-security prisons now feature. In "Inside the New High-Tech Lock-Downs," Jim Rendon examines the role that technology plays in prison design. Innovations such as tracking devices, remote monitoring screens, intercoms, and TV-screen teleconferencing—which in some prisons replaces face-to-face visits—minimize inmates' human contact. Technology has allowed prisons to cut the ratio of guards to prisoners by approximately half since the 1960s.

In "U.S. 'Supermax' Prisons Incite Human Rights Outcry," Alan Elsner visits the new high-security, or "supermax," prisons that currently house about 20,000 inmates in the U.S. Reports of harsh, isolated conditions, suicides, and assaults on inmates by guards have stirred debate about supermax prisons.

Supporters argue that these prisons remove the most dangerous prisoners from lower-security prisons and ease constraints on those prisoners who are less inclined to violence.

Prisoner's Dilemma[1]

By Michael Berryhill
New Republic, December 27, 1999

Sometimes a crime is so despicable that it defines, at least for a time, the place where it occurs. Think of Oklahoma City, or Littleton, Colorado—or Jasper, an East Texas logging town where, in June of last year, a black man named James Byrd Jr. was chained by his ankles to the bumper of a pickup truck and dragged three miles down country roads. His knees and his genitalia were ground off. When he hit a culvert, his head and one shoulder were severed from his body. His corpse was deposited near the gate of a black cemetery where former slaves were buried and where some of the bodies were memorialized with spirit markers, in keeping with ancient African tradition.

The murder thrust Jasper into the national glare, and at first its moral seemed clear. The cotton and timber country of East Texas, the media noted, had always been known for its racism. During Jim Crow, most of the state's lynchings took place there. One of the last bastions of the Ku Klux Klan had its headquarters in Vidor, 70 miles south of Jasper. It wasn't hard to see what the Jasper killing meant. It meant that, in the poor, hick towns of the Deep South, white people hadn't really changed.

Then, over time, the story shifted. Two days after the murder, Jasper County Sheriff Billy Rowles picked up three local white men: John William King, Lawrence Russell Brewer, and Shawn Berry. A judge refused to move the first case, King's, from Jasper, saying the town could deal with its own. By February of this year, an almost entirely white jury of townspeople had convicted King of murder and sentenced him to death, making him only the second white man in Texas history to be given the death penalty for the murder of an African-American. After the verdict was announced, Rowles, a slow-talking white man in his fifties, embraced Byrd's son before the cameras. A TV reporter who covered King's trial told me he felt something "almost spiritual" upon hearing that King had been condemned to death. Jasper was not the Old South after all.

Two more trials and two more convictions followed, with Brewer also getting the death penalty and Berry receiving a life sentence just a few weeks ago. Now Jasper is receding from sight. The town,

---

1. Article by Michael Berryhill from *The New Republic* December 27, 1999. Copyright © *The New Republic*. Reprinted with permission

too, had been on trial, and, to the surprise of many, it has been found innocent. By moving so swiftly and decisively to find the killers and bring them to justice, Jasper proved it was not responsible for King and Brewer and Berry, after all. With the morality play resolved, the national media has gone home, leaving just one question, a question no one seemed to want to ask: If Jasper did not create the killers of James Byrd, what did?

Although Bill King, Russell Brewer, and Shawn Berry were all convicted of James Byrd's murder, it eventually became apparent that Berry's role had been markedly different from King's or Brewer's. Even the prosecution admitted that Berry was not a racist. Indeed, at his trial, several black coworkers testified that Berry had good relations with them. Berry was, however, a high school friend of King's. That's why King and Brewer, an old friend of King's from prison, were in Berry's truck the night they picked up Byrd, who had been hitchhiking. Berry said King and Brewer ordered him to stop the truck on a remote dirt road, whereupon they pulled Byrd out of the cab and began beating him. Paralyzed with fear, Berry said, he wet his pants and did nothing to stop them.

> *Three working-class white men grew up in small East Texas towns. . . . [Two] went into Texas prisons, and one did not. And the two who did came out monsters.*

In contrast to Berry, both King and Brewer were avowed white supremacists, their bodies covered with racist tattoos. They didn't get the tattoos in Jasper; they got them in prison. While Berry, as a teenager, had been arrested along with King for stealing cigarettes from a warehouse, he had served time only in a boot camp for young offenders. After that, Berry kept his nose clean and stayed out of jail. King, on the other hand, violated his probation and was soon sent to prison, where he met Brewer. It was that experience that made King and Brewer the men they are today. Three working-class white men grew up in small East Texas towns at about the same time and under similar conditions. Two went into Texas prisons, and one did not. And the two who did came out monsters.

King and Brewer called themselves "woods." In the racial war that goes on in Texas prisons, where inmates of color outnumber whites by about three to one, "wood" is short for "peckerwood." Black Southerners started using the word peckerwood to refer to poor whites some time at the end of the last century. Blacks, writes Clarence Major in his dictionary of African-American slang, "saw the common blackbird as a symbol of themselves." The redheaded woodpeckers that roamed the Southern forests came to represent whites.

And, just as blacks have so often appropriated the epithets of whites, whites in Texas prisons have adopted peckerwood and made it their own.

In Texas prisons, a wood is a white man who will "stay down," or fight for himself and his friends. If he's a good fighter, he is known as a "hard wood." If he caves in, goes fetal, calls for the guards, weeps, pleads, or fails to fight, he's a "ho," a whore, suitable for extortion and rape. Ho's are the lowest men in the prison hierarchy, despised by inmates and guards alike. When inmates fail to defend themselves against sexual assault, the common advice of prison authorities is to "act like a man."

King and Brewer met at the Beto unit of the Texas Department of Criminal Justice in 1995. Beto is considered by inmates to be a "gladiator" unit: 3,000 young men in their twenties, many of them toughened by living on the streets and as members of racial gangs.

Prison victims come in all colors and sizes, of course, but young whites, prison officials and defense lawyers say, have an especially hard time. A middle-class white boy sent to prison for trying to stretch his allowance by dealing drugs or breaking into houses may have to fight day after day. He will be attacked not only because he inspires resentment but because such attacks can be lucrative. More than half of Texas inmates are broke. Although inmates are required to work in the fields, factories, and offices of Texas prisons, Texas pays them nothing for their labor. So inmates find other ways to make money. One is to sell contraband—tobacco, drugs, pornography—that is often smuggled in by the poorly paid guards. Another way is through extortion. Still another is by turning a prisoner into a ho and selling his sexual services to other inmates.

Trying to account for what happened to their client in prison, King's lawyers put a Beto inmate named John Mosley on the stand. A towering man, six-foot-three and 280 pounds, Mosley gave King many of his racist tattoos. In response to questions from King's lawyers, Mosley told the jury about a common practice in Texas prisons, known as "checking," by which inmates vet new arrivals. Asked what checking is, Mosley explained matter-of-factly, "It means you fight, fuck, or 'up sixties;" referring to the $60-a-month maximum that an inmate could at that time spend at the commissary. If an inmate gives in, he becomes a ho and can be "rented" to other prisoners, a profitable enterprise.

King never testified, and prison records indicate next to nothing about whether or how King was checked, except that he was in a scuffle on his first day, in June 1995. Whatever happened, though, it must have scared him—for he soon joined his cellmate Brewer's small white gang, the Confederate Knights of America, for protection.

Brewer, though a few years older than King, was a man much like him. A small-town burglar who sometimes stole from his own relatives, Brewer was in and out of prison for seven years. Like King, Brewer was relatively small in size and, except for his tattoos, was hardly intimidating.

During his trial, Brewer described in weeping, halting testimony how he had come to join the Confederate Knights. Soon after he arrived at Beto, in early 1994, Brewer was checked by two Hispanic gang members. The guards, he said, had ordered all the inmates in his cellblock to sit down on benches in the dayroom or be punished. It was almost as if the guards wanted to see what confrontation would transpire. Blacks held one bench, Hispanics held another, and whites occupied the third—but the whites wouldn't let Brewer

---

Brewer and King each acquired a multitude of racist tattoos—created by other inmates using a needle hooked to a small electrical motor pilfered from a typewriter or a light fixture.

---

sit with them. For two days, he said, he leaned against the wall. Then two Hispanic gang members asked him whether he would fight or "ride"—that is, give them money or sexual favors. Brewer said he told them he would not ride and if they were going to beat him up they should go ahead and get it over with.

As far as checking goes, Brewer had it easy—the two Hispanics never made good on their threat. Still, his fellow white inmates were sufficiently impressed with his refusal to back down that they allowed him to sit on their bench. And Brewer was soon invited to join the Confederate Knights.

The Confederate Knights was a fledgling group, in contrast to better-established white gangs at Beto such as the Aryan Circle and the Aryan Brotherhood. The Beto chapter called itself the Texas Rebel Soldiers; its members swore oaths of loyalty to the Ku Klux Klan. Prison authorities and King's lawyers say no more than a dozen inmates were members. With typical exaggeration, King bragged in a letter to a girlfriend that "not just anyone is prospected and asked to be a part of these brotherhoods. One must be one down motherfuckin' peckerwood. Any white boy who comes in and stays down for himself is a wood or peckerwood. That's when you receive your bolts [tattooed SS lighting bolts] and nickname."

In addition to the bolts, Brewer and King each acquired a multitude of racist tattoos—created by other inmates using a needle hooked to a small electrical motor pilfered from a typewriter or a light fixture. King was particularly proud of a menacing version of Woody Woodpecker dressed in a Klan robe and perched on a limb from which dangled the tiny figure of a hanged black man. He wrote to a girlfriend that he was friends with "one of the coldest skin artist[s] on this unit. "Hopefully by the time I come home," he wrote, "I'll have 65 percent of my body covered. My head, arms, neck, back, side, chest, stomach and dick. I know no one's gonna want to fuck with a . . . peckerwood covered in skin art."

Being a member of the Confederate Knights meant sharing the secret password, attending meetings, acting as a lookout, hiding documents, earning points on a merit chart, and swearing to "bear true allegiance to the sacred principles of Aryan Racial Supremacy and political freedom in Government upon which our forefathers founded a new nation upon this continent. Most importantly, it gave men like King someone to call "bro" (another word, like ho and peckerwood, that prison whites took from the people they said they hated).

Misfits in the small towns where they grew up, in prison King and Brewer found a group that accepted them. Brewer cut short the visits of his Hispanic wife and son for fear of antagonizing his fellow gang members. His brothers in prison were more important, he testified. Bound by rituals, tattoos, and written oaths sealed with bloody thumbprints, they were initiates to a secret order. They had a common enemy: the "mud race."

By becoming woods, Brewer's and King's lawyers argued, the two men didn't just protect themselves from the theft of their commissary money. They protected themselves from rape. In describing his checking experience, Brewer stated that "the odds [of being raped] were against me looking like I did with no tattoos." King, however, refused to help his lawyers present fear of rape as a mitigating circumstance for his racist views. C. Haden Cribbs, one of King's lawyers, says that when he asked King if he had been sexually assaulted, King got "positively indignant" and wouldn't talk about the subject. Ultimately, the jury didn't buy the rationale, and neither, for the most part, did the press. At one of the defense team's daily news conferences, one reporter chided King's other lawyer, Brack Jones, with the comment that "[the prison] system isn't on trial." . . .

Meanwhile, membership in prison gangs continues to rise. According to Sam Buentello, chief of the Texas prison system's gang-intelligence unit, about 5,000 inmates are known to belong to officially recognized gangs, with another 10,000 suspected of gang affiliations. About 700 belong to the white supremacist groups Aryan Brotherhood or Aryan Circle. About 900 belong to either the Crips or the Bloods, the black gangs. The greatest number belong to Hispanic gangs, such as the Mexican Mafia and the Texas Syndicate. These recognized gangs elect officers, take votes, conduct courts, and execute punishments in a legalistic manner, with communications coded or sometimes hidden in legal papers that prison authorities are forbidden by law to intercept and read.

Compared to the major gangs, King and Brewer's Confederate Knights of America was small potatoes. It didn't have a written constitution, and the Texas Department of Criminal Justice termed it not a gang but a clique. Yet it clearly made an impact on both King and Brewer.

After he joined, King's letters from prison to his girlfriends became increasingly racist—and were often tinged with sexual resentment of minorities. Woods were always the victims of prison authority. Blacks and Hispanics got away with everything. "Truthfully sweetheart," he wrote, "sometimes I just feel like 'fuck comeing home.' I'm better off here. I have it made in all actuality, why give it up for a world full of nothing? What do I have to look forward too returning to Jasper? A town full of race traitoring nigger loveing whores? Bitches that are so fuckin stupid and blind to the pride of their race and heritiage that they should be hung on the limb adjacent their nigger loveing man."

When they were finally released from prison in 1997, King and Brewer brought their racism home with them. When King first returned to Jasper, his old pal Shawn Berry said, he spouted racist talk and displayed his tattoos. But, according to Berry, King toned it down when he didn't get any response from Berry and his friends and started wearing long-sleeved shirts to cover up the tattoos. Then, three weeks before Byrd's murder, Brewer—who had been thrown out of the house he'd been sharing with a girlfriend in a small town north of Jasper—moved in with King.

According to Berry, when Brewer showed up, the two former cellmates returned to their prison slang and took up their old ways. When they needed a chain saw and a weed trimmer for a job clearing brush, they stole them. They took 50 bags of potato chips from a motel lobby. When they wanted beer, they broke into a warehouse and took a dozen cases. A few nights before killing Byrd, they cleaned out a restaurant's supply of frozen steaks.

They also revived their commitment to the Confederate Knights. King even wanted to start a chapter in Jasper. In his apartment, police found membership forms and a written constitution for the gang.

Berry contends he never believed King or Brewer would act on their racism, but he admits the two were outspoken about it. Indeed, on the afternoon before Byrd's murder, King had been angry about encountering blacks at two different parties at friends' homes.

Brewer and King also seemed obsessed with asserting their masculinity and repudiating homosexuality. The constitution of the Confederate Knights expressly forbids homosexuality. In prison, King had gotten a tattoo of the Disney character Tinkerbell on his penis, and he showed it off to several of Berry's friends one night at the movie theater that Berry managed. Brewer also said that on the night of the murder he and King got out of the truck and were relieving themselves in the clearing when King tried to "bum" him— prison slang, Brewer politely explained to the jury, "for trying to get me to look at his thing." Such sexual horseplay between Brewer and King was common. The two sometimes tweaked each other's breasts and teased each other about "getting it" from a black cellmate. The two men's racism, in short, seems intimately tied to their sexual fears.

It is telling, then, that Byrd's torture and killing included an element of sexual humiliation. Before chaining Byrd to the bumper, King and Brewer pulled down his pants. And, after the dragging was over and the trio was driving back to Jasper, Berry says King told him, "that's what they did to niggers when they messed with white women in the old days." But who was the white woman who felt sexually threatened by Byrd? It may have been King.

Of course nothing King and Brewer experienced in prison justifies what they did. And, although their tattoos made them look tough, they were cowards. The man they killed was helpless and drunk. It is also true that many white inmates who join racist gangs in prison manage to leave them once they get out.

But the fact remains that the kind of racially motivated sexual torture and murder that King and Brewer committed is common enough in Texas prisons that, had they carried out a similar crime while still in jail, it would scarcely have been noticed. By committing it on the outside, King and Brewer have opened a window onto what happens on a frequent basis in Texas's vast prison system. And, as an estimated 300,000 men like King and Brewer are released from the Texas prison system over the next ten years, it is entirely possible—indeed, likely—that we will see more and more racially motivated, prison-style crimes outside prison walls. Just last month, police say, a white teenager who had been in several juvenile facilities in Indiana shot and killed a black teenager in order to gain status within a white supremacist prison gang.

King, for his part, appears to have gotten the verdict he wanted. In a prison "kite," or note, that King sent to Brewer before their trials, King seems to have hoped to die a martyr to the cause of white supremacy. Indignant that Brewer testified that they were both at the murder scene, King has thrown Brewer out of the Confederate Knights of America, one of King's lawyers said. And, on the afternoon King was sentenced to death, the press asked him whether he had anything to say to Byrd's family. He replied, with a smirk, "They can suck my dick."

Last spring, while a hundred or so reporters and photographers waited for the jury to announce King's sentence, I drove to a state park on the edge of town to listen to the local radio station and breathe some fresh air. After a two-and-a-half-hour deliberation, the jury returned the death penalty. I looked up and a solitary pileated woodpecker swooped unhurriedly through the pines, its red topknot distinct and pointed. When the radio reporter interviewed Jasper citizens on the sidewalk, several of them said that, for the murderers of James Byrd, death was an easy way out. Life in prison, they reasoned, would have been worse.

Inside the New High-Tech Lock-Downs[2]

BY JIM RENDON
SALON.COM, SEPTEMBER 8, 1998

In a small, dim room where riot gear is chained to the wall and a computer monitor is perched on the counter, three jail guards sit comfortably behind tall tinted windows, keeping order on the cell block below them without lifting a boot. The recreation room, jail cells and showers arc in a neat semicircle around the control booth. Cell doors are open since it is recreation time, and the inmates, wearing Los Angeles County's gold and royal blue uniforms, play checkers and talk in the day room, an open area near the cells. Instead of bars, shatter-proof glass walls confine the inmates—leaving guards and prisoners to eye each other mutely all day long, like fish in neighboring tanks on a pet store shelf.

"Lock down, possible miss out in the facility," a voice crackles over the booth's intercom. Somewhere in the building an inmate is missing. No one moves except officer Johnson. He casually flips a switch on the control panel, and a loud siren begins to wail. Then he bends the microphone toward his mouth. "All inmates in 151, all inmates in 151, lock down, lock down," he chants in a cheerful singsong voice. "Start closing all cell doors, we're locking down, gentlemen," he finishes, easing back from the microphone.

The trio of guards look on from their perch as the 192 inmates on this floor break up their conversations and amble toward the two-tiered wall of cells on their own. There is no need for the guards to leave the booth. If anything looks suspicious, the officers can flip a switch to eavesdrop on any of the 96 cells, or talk privately with an inmate from the comfort of their post. Although a video camera points toward the day room, ready to document any trouble that might arise, nothing transpires—the inmates seem more resigned than defiant. Once in their cells, the prisoners close the solid doors and wait to hear the bolt slide into place, as the guards in the control booth move lever after lever.

When each door is secured, lights on the booth's console flicker from red to green, indicating who is locked in. Only after all doors are sealed will the guards leave their posts to peer through the small glass windows in each cell door, visually identifying and counting inmates.

This is life in the Twin Towers, Los Angeles County's high-tech lock up. The sleek new building is the first of what is being hailed as a new generation of jails—facilities that combine technology and innovative design to help contain the cost of jailing people while further isolating and controlling them. Fueled by decades of anti-crime rhetoric, inmate populations have boomed in recent years—from 500,000 in 1980 to 1.8 million in 1997—and pushed prison capacity to the breaking point. Today, with the help of high-tech solutions, prisons are now locking up more prisoners using fewer guards—and at the same time furthering the trend toward less rehabilitation and more punishment.

In the early 1980s, California pioneered the effort to funnel new technology into prisons. Last year, the state became the first to use a new inmate monitoring system that, according to its creator, revolutionizes the way prisons are run.

Jim Ricketts, president and founder of Technology Systems International, is part of a new generation of entrepreneurs seeking fortunes in corrections technology. He left a successful career at the Colorado Department of Corrections to found his own company in Scottsdale, Ariz. Ricketts thought he could use his lifetime of experience to cash in on the high-tech rush. He took an idea to Motorola and left with PRISM, the Prison Inmate and Safety Management System. PRISM is designed to reduce the amount of time guards spend counting prisoners—a face-to-face visual identification process that has changed little in the last 100 years.

In a PRISM prison, each inmate wears a wrist band that looks like an oversized digital watch. Guards wear devices that look like beepers. Both gadgets emit a radio signal every two seconds that is received by nodes located throughout the prison and yard, enabling the system to continuously tally inmates. The signal carries identifying characteristics that allow PRISM to recognize individuals. By recording the location of the node and the time difference between signal receptions, the system allows each prisoner's location to be noted and monitored all day, every day. This information is digitally archived and stored for up to a week. If violence breaks out, guards can find out who was in the area and use that information in court. A schedule for every inmate can also be entered in the system so PRISM, like an omnipresent truant officer, can ensure that everyone is in the right place at the right time. If an inmate blocks the signal or takes the band off, PRISM will make sure that someone comes looking.

Ricketts is proud of his system but aware that such persistent monitoring can have a dark side as well. "A system like this can be tightened down so much that it can drive the inmates crazy," he admits. "Normally we recommend allowing inmates some latitude."

At Salinas Valley State Prison, a huge, low complex that almost disappears into the flat, brown agricultural landscape an hour south of San Jose, a computer-monitored lethal electric fence

> *Technology . . . is increasingly seen as the answer to America's prison crisis.*

encircles the prison's perimeter. In place at more than 20 California prisons, this gulag-style inmate catcher has become a statewide favorite. The 5,100-volt current that courses through the wires is more than double the jolt given by Florida's infamous electric chair, Old Sparky. Gus Meza, the plant supervisor for the prison, says the fence is so effective that 11 of 13 guard towers can be left unoccupied, saving Salinas Valley $1 million a year in staffing costs.

At first glance a lethal fence seems extreme, a harking back to some of the darker pages in modern history. But given the intrusive nature of the microphones, video cameras and stage-like showers that grace many new prisons and jails, the fence strikes a strangely benign note. Sandwiched between two chain-link fences that are topped with loops of razor wire, the 15 electrified wires hang no more than a foot apart. Any movement of the wire, or variation in the current, will trigger an alarm—and a lethal jolt. Guards in the command center watch a graphic representation of the fenced perimeter that instantly pinpoints any change in current; the same system also sends a message to the watch commander's beeper in the event of an incident. So far, the fence has worked—no one has yet escaped over or under it.

Technology like this is increasingly seen as the answer to America's prison crisis. While inmate populations have ballooned at every level of the justice system, spending, though growing as well, has not kept pace. Governments are scrambling to meet the needs of money-hungry corrections departments. Since staffing costs will eventually balloon beyond a prison's original price tag, and employees account for 65 percent of a prison's operating budget, jobs are an obvious target for cuts. "You fight for operating budgets year after year, which is why staff is often cut back," explains Steve Carter, president of Carter Goble Associates, a prison consulting firm. "You only have to negotiate for your capital budget once." That makes it easier to invest in technology over people—even if it does come at the cost of angering California's politically potent prison guard lobby.

Not everyone thinks that prison is the place for high-tech supervision. "Technology is working against what jails should be doing," says Dr. Richard Wener, an environmental psychologist with the Polytechnic University in Brooklyn, N.Y. Wener, who has studied prisons for 20 years and regularly consults on new corrections designs, is frustrated by the Twin Towers approach. "High-tech supervision," he says, "is not the most effective way to run a jail; it is not safer, not less stressful, not a better opportunity for rehabilitation or education." Wener wants to tear down the control booth and put guards back on the floor where they can get to know inmates. He advocates direct supervision—the jailhouse equivalent of community policing. "When you are on the floor, you can stop a fight before it starts," he says. "When you are observing from a distance, all you can do is break up the fight after it has begun."

Even family members' visits are now channeled through a TV screen, thanks to the magic of teleconferencing.

But rehabilitation is rarely a concern anymore, says Jennie Gainsborough, a spokeswoman for the National Prison Project of the American Civil Liberties Union. Popular attitudes toward imprisonment have become more punitive. And as politicians get further into the business of dictating how inmates will be managed, prison environments have become increasingly restrictive, often with the help of new technology. Carter is also well aware of the problems. "In some instances, technology is being used to ensure that inmates live in total isolation," he says. Corrections officials bug cells, talk to inmates over speakers and beam what classes are available to TVs placed outside cells; even family members' visits are now channeled through a TV screen, thanks to the magic of teleconferencing. "What effect do you think this would have on you?" Gainsborough asks. "Would it contribute to mental health, or increase social problems?"

Her question, like Wener's solution, has been largely ignored during the recent prison-construction boom. While direct supervision was the hot new trend 15 years ago, today, high-tech circular designs dominate the punitive cutting edge. Chief Barry King, who runs Twin Towers, is convinced that the round design of the jail, coupled with its reliance on technology, is the only thing that makes the 4,000-bed, maximum security jail affordable to operate. "In an old jail, everything was designed in blocks—you needed more people to walk the rows of cells. Over here, you can have one guard watch the whole area," he says, gesturing at the stylish new jail that rises outside his window.

To develop efficient plans for people like King, designers have looked all the way back to Jeremy Bentham, the 18th-century British utilitarian philosopher and grandfather of the hottest trend in prison design today. Bentham, a social reformer, drew up plans for his ideal prison, the panopticon—a circular cell-house with a central guard station where a few officers could watch over hundreds of inmates stacked many stories high. Prison administrators following Bentham believed that the specter of constant surveillance would make prisoners more apt to follow rules and help them integrate into society when they were released. Bentham's plan also required fewer guards—a fact that has not been lost on today's prison designers.

Charles Oraftik runs the criminal justice division of Hellmuth Obata and Kassabaum, the San Francisco architectural firm that designed the Twin Towers. He points to the circular prison plan in front of him, noting the ease with which inmates can be viewed by a single, centrally placed guard. Because staffing costs can far outstrip a prison's original price tag, designers are now under intense pressure to dream up buildings that allow fewer staff to control ever larger numbers of inmates. "The most important thing is to be secure and efficient. If your building is not efficient, it can cost you," Oraftik says. Improving sight lines from the control booth to the prison floor and into every cell is the key to keeping guard-to-inmate ratios low.

In the 1960s, the guard-to-prisoner ratio was 1-to-30. Now, 1-to-60 is common. Some prisons, like one Oraftik is working on in a remote part of Oregon, have a ratio of 1-to-100. "We can make the architecture so efficient that the limits fade," he says with pride. "We are not limited by architecture, but by human capability. Eventually the staff burns out. You can allow them to see even more than they can process."

Along with changing their designs, prisons administrators are using technology to help them isolate what they consider problem inmates from the general population, creating prisons within the prison system. This is not a particularly new development—the trend began as far back as the 1930s, at Alcatraz, the desolate island penitentiary in San Francisco Bay. Alcatraz's first warden, James Johnson, created a prison far ahead of its time. He directed everything from the use of pastel colors—which he thought would calm inmates long before studies proved it so—to elaborate safety precautions and procedures.

At Alcatraz, guns and keys were kept in elevated caged walkways that lined the walls at the north and south ends of the main cellblock. Armed guards watched over the entire floor from these perches, rather than walking the floor where inmates could grab weapons. Keys were lowered on a string only when needed. Alcatraz added electrically operated remote control doors to the isolation units in 1940, and early metal detectors, which inmates called snitch boxes, scanned prisoners twice a day. At every point as they were shuffled from work to meals and back to their cells, inmates were tallied, watched and searched.

> "*Supermax is the flavor of the decade.*" —Steve Carter, president of Carter Goble Associates

After Alcatraz closed in the 1960s, the government dumped troublesome federal inmates into the general prison population. Twenty years of this proved enough for the feds, and in the 1980s they once again began to sequester problem inmates—this time at Marion prison in Illinois. Administrators dreamed up a whole new kind of prison, a place where inmates were confined to their cells up to 22 and a half hours a day as part of their regular routine.

Marion, and prisons like it that have sprung up around the country, rely on surveillance and remote-control technology to monitor and supervise inmates while isolating them. Using even basic technology, it is possible to move an inmate from his cell to the yard and back again without ever coming in contact with him. Plummeting prices and the increased sophistication of surveillance and computer technology have made it possible to replicate "supermax" prisons like Marion elsewhere, for less cost.

As surveillance has became more accepted, state and even local governments have gotten into the game, says Stephen Ingley, director of the American Jail Association. "The technology is everywhere. It has become easier to find and cheaper to buy," he says. In 1980 there were no supermax prisons in the United States; the phrase had yet to be coined. Now there are 50 supermax prisons, and more on the way. California's three units house 2,700 of its 154,000 inmates. "Supermax is the flavor of the decade," says Carter.

But the prison of choice in the 1990s has not been without its problems. In 1995, the California Department of Corrections lost a major class-action suit over the nightmarish conditions at the Pelican Bay State Prison's supermax facility, known as the Secure Housing Unit (SHU).

Opened in 1989, Pelican Bay has been a long-running scandal for the Department of Corrections. Prisoners are not relegated to the SHU because of the crimes they committed on the outside, but because of the rules they broke on the inside. And placement in the SHU is often for the duration of a prisoner's sentence. The 8-by-10-foot cells have no windows. The walls are white, and all that can be seen through the perforations in each cell's metal door is another white wall. Many inmates do not have televisions or radios. And, as at Marion, they are kept in their cells 22 and a half hours a day. Guards perched in control booths can open and close doors and communicate with inmates without ever leaving their seats. Human contact is minimal.

"It's like a space capsule where one is shot into space and left in isolation," said one inmate who testified in the suit. Significant numbers of inmates had mental problems that were exacerbated by the high-tech isolation inside the SHU. They experienced audio or visual distortions and outright hallucinations, aggressive fantasies, paranoia or problems controlling their impulses. Suicide attempts and violent outbursts were regular occurrences. Guard-on-inmate violence skyrocketed.

Despite its problems, Pelican Bay has become a model for dozens of supermax prisons popping up around the country. Louisiana now has three supermax prisons; Pennsylvania has two; Washington state, three. And now, the Twin Towers has become the first facility to bring the supermax concept all the way down to the county jail level—where most inmates have yet to be convicted of anything and are still awaiting trial.

Though the Twin Towers houses only maximum security inmates, a few of the jail's floors have been set aside for what King calls "high-power" inmates—people deemed to be so dangerous that they must spend even their recreation time locked in a cage. On most floors in the jail, the recreation yards are open spaces with basketball hoops and pay phones; but on the isolation floors, no one is going to shoot hoops. The space is occupied by four 8-by-10-foot cages, each equipped with a jail phone. The cages are staggered diagonally across the floor so one guard can watch all the inmates. Sgt. Andres Ramirez explains that high-power inmates are required by law to have time in the yard. But because of their classification, they must also be separated from other prisoners at all times. "This," Ramirez says, his hand resting on the cage, "qualifies as exposure to outside recreation." His voice is clear, without a hint of irony.

On the second floor of the Twin Towers, a crowd of employees has gathered at a window that looks into the building's command center. The passage to freedom is adjacent to this bustling nerve center so guards can visually identify people moving in and out of the secure area. Inside, guards dash frantically about, bumping shoulders in the tight space, answering phone calls and responding to requests to open doors, move elevators or change ventilation patterns. They flash a quick look at a video monitor or bark into a microphone to ensure that they are not letting the wrong person pass through a door or an elevator. Occasionally a guard glances at the growing crowd waiting at the door, but amid the insistent buzzing they can do little more than shrug apologetically. It will be a while.

When the door finally opens, I walk down a long hallway past row after row of gun lockers, heading steadily toward the exit sign. At the end of the hall a door leads to a metal staircase painted in tasteful teal. I soon find myself on an empty, glass-enclosed landing. The only door leads outside. I suddenly begin to wonder if the door will open, if I will be allowed to get out—after all, it is a jail. I reach out to push the latch, expecting to find it locked. But the instant before I make contact, I hear a heavy metallic clang; the mechanism is unlocked and the door swings wide.

Outside, I take a deep breath. I want to walk quickly to my car and flee this corner of Los Angeles, but I can't resist one last look. As the door slowly shuts, I catch a glimpse of a small window facing me in the wall about 10 feet up. Behind the glass, I can make out the sleepless eye of a video camera.

U.S. "Supermax" Prisons Incite Human Rights Outcry[3]

By Alan Elsner
Los Angeles Times, March 11, 2001

Imagine being locked alone in a small, bare cell for 23 hours a day. Your meals are slid through a slot in the metal door. You cannot see or talk to another human being. You cannot see out the window.

You cannot make telephone calls or have direct contact with visitors. When you do briefly leave your cell for showers or solitary exercise, you must strip and permit a visual search of your body, including bending over and spreading your buttocks. Your legs are shackled, your arms are cuffed and you are led by two guards, one of whom presses an electric stun gun against your body at all times.

Such conditions are typical in so-called "supermaximum security prisons"—the hottest trend in the U.S. prison system—which now house at least 20,000 inmates.

Popular with politicians, supermax prisons are under increasing scrutiny in lawsuits and official investigations probing persistent allegations of serious human rights excesses.

Supermax prisons are designed for what corrections officials call the "worst of the worst"—prisoners so violent, so disruptive, so incorrigible that they cannot be kept in regular custody. Politicians who want to be seen as tough on crime have championed the construction of such facilities, which cost considerably more to build and operate than regular prisons.

But human rights organizations and a growing number of independent experts say many of those locked up are not violent or dangerous criminals but seriously mentally ill individuals.

Sometimes, nonviolent offenders who have never caused trouble can get shunted into supermax facilities because it would be embarrassing to the authorities, having constructed such expensive prisons, to leave them half empty.

A report by Human Rights Watch said, "The conditions of confinement impose pointless suffering and humiliation. The absence of normal human interaction, of reasonable mental stimulus, of almost anything that makes life bearable, is emotionally, physically and psychologically destructive."

---

3. Copyright © Reuters Limited 2001.

The Justice Department is investigating conditions in Virginia supermaxes after two prisoners transferred from Connecticut died under suspicious circumstances.

One, a young drug offender, committed suicide seven months before his release date. The other, a diabetic, went into convulsions after allegedly being denied his medication. Guards reacted by firing their stun guns at him, and he later died.

The Virginia Department of Corrections said an investigation found that the firing of the stun guns had nothing to do with his death and the guards had acted properly.

In another lawsuit, 108 prisoners from New Mexico who were sent to the Wallens Ridge supermax in Virginia alleged they were systematically beaten, shocked with stun guns and terrorized by

---

Since Virginia opened its two supermaxes, assaults on staff and other inmates have dropped by nearly half in the state's other prisons.

---

guards who taunted them with racial epithets. The FBI was looking into these allegations.

A Virginia spokesman declined to respond but said Corrections Commissioner Ron Angelone would be willing to do so in an interview at some unspecified time in the future.

In June 2000 Angelone testified before a Virginia commission, "I'm a little angry with all of this. This is the same garbage that I heard from New Mexico—lies from convicted felons who don't like being locked up in tough prisons."

He said that since Virginia opened its two supermaxes, assaults on staff and other inmates have dropped by nearly half in the state's other prisons.

In Illinois, four prisoners at the Tamms supermax who say they are seriously mentally ill have brought a class action lawsuit alleging cruel and unusual punishment through "sensory deprivation based on near-total isolation."

One inmate, Ashoor Rasho, became so desperate and disturbed that, according to the court complaint, "on Aug. 20, 1998, with his arms already infected from self-inflicted wounds, Mr. Rasho again cut his arm and began eating small pieces of his own flesh in front of a correctional officer."

The officer allegedly ignored the medical emergency and also ignored Rasho's plea to speak to someone from the mental health unit. Rasho was eventually stitched up and returned to the same cell, where he cut himself again, pulled his stitches out and lost more than half a pint of blood.

A spokesman for the Illinois Department of Corrections said he would be eager to respond to written questions. A week after they were submitted, he had not done so.

In Ohio the American Civil Liberties Union filed a federal civil rights action citing conditions that led to at least three inmate suicides in the Youngstown supermax, where psychotherapy is conducted with prisoners chained to a pole.

The Ohio Corrections Department says those in Youngstown are "the predators, the guys who have attacked inmates or guards, the people who need to be separated from the rest of the system."

Chase Riveland, who headed the Washington state prison system for 11 years and Colorado's for four years, said he was extremely concerned at the proliferation of supermax prisons.

"We don't know what we're doing to these people and what they will do to us when they return to their communities, which most of them eventually will do," he said.

Indiana State University criminologist Robert Huckabee, who conducted a study of supermaxes for the state of Indiana, said there had been little scientific study of the long-term effects of such incarceration on inmates.

While generally defending the use of supermaxes for extremely dangerous or disruptive prisoners, Huckabee said the heavy presence of the mentally ill was an "issue of concern."

"If we don't want mentally ill people in our prisons, we need to ask our judges to stop sending them and our legislatures to provide the money for other facilities," he said.

VI. Unlocking Doors: Alternatives to Prison

Inmates discuss their concerns at a substance abuse program meeting of a Special Unit for AIDS patients at the Limestone Correctional Facility in Capshaw, Alabama.

Editor's Introduction

Are there ways of dealing with criminals other than, or in addition to, putting them behind bars? Depending on the nature of the crime, various methods are either currently in use or being proposed. For nonviolent offenders, some lower courts—and recently some federal courts—have opted for public shaming, forcing criminals to advertise their guilt. For those convicted of drug-related crimes, institutions are increasingly turning to drug rehabilitation as an alterative to prison. Such methods reduce the prison population and may serve as well as or better than prison to eliminate addicts' dependency on drugs. Finally, restorative justice has been introduced in many states for both nonviolent and violent criminals. Usually implemented in addition to prison time, restorative justice impels criminals to acknowledge the harm they have caused and allows them to make reparations to their victims or the victims' families. In such cases victims are not obliged to accept apologies, though some have found that it helps to heal their wounds.

Section VI begins with "Restoring Dignity, Effecting Justice," in which David Lerman outlines the principles of restorative justice. Lerman cites several successful examples, including the case of a young cashier convicted of stealing from the store where she worked who agreed to speak about her experience at orientation sessions for new employees, and an incident involving two young people who spray-painted neo-Nazi graffiti on a synagogue. A four-hour meeting between the latter two offenders and members of the synagogue revealed the depths of the youths' ignorance, and in lieu of a prison sentence, they were allowed to repair some of the damage they had done, while learning more about the people they had mistreated.

Lisa Singhania looks at several modern-day versions of *The Scarlet Letter* in "Courts Turning to Public Shaming of Wrongdoers." She reports that public shaming—making offenders place ads, wear placards, or display bumper stickers proclaiming their guilt—is starting to be used for nonviolent offenders in federal courts. This embarrassing procedure appears to deter some forms of criminal behavior; whether it rehabilitates criminals is under debate.

On July 1, 2001, California passed Proposition 36, which prescribes rehabilitation rather than prison time for California's estimated 36,000 nonviolent drug offenders each year. It is still uncertain how well rehabilitation will work, but in "Old Habits, New Hopes," Patrick Rogers, Ron Arias, and Maureen Harrington report on Impact, a particularly successful drug rehabilitation center. Seventy percent of Impact's clients complete the program and remain arrest-free, they note.

Finally, in "A New Model to Deal with Crime and Its Victims: Forgiveness," Jane Lampman looks at some of the roughly 300 programs in the U.S. criminal justice system that focus on forgiveness. While citing cases in which victims have forgiven offenders—such as a woman who was shot and partially paralyzed by a young man—Lampman wonders whether forgiveness might be a key to rehabilitating both criminals and their victims.

Restoring Dignity, Effecting Justice[1]

BY DAVID LERMAN
HUMAN RIGHTS, FALL 1999

Human rights activists have long focused their struggles on the people affected by various criminal justice systems. Although these efforts have often born fruit in individual cases and have perhaps affected some small changes that have long-term impact in particular systems, these efforts fail to look at the "big picture." A deeper analysis of that picture reveals that Western-based modes of meting out criminal justice fail to take into account the fundamental human right of being interconnected with one another in healthy communities. The U.S. criminal justice system, for instance, has the wrong focus—punishing convicted criminals by putting them behind bars.

The ripple effects of the social isolation caused by crime are numerous. We lose the capacity to resolve disputes on our own. We lose our capacity to see ourselves as part of a "we," and become less willing to participate in social movements working with and trusting others.

In this sense, crime is not just an offense against an individual, it is an offense against the whole social fabric of the country. The current criminal justice focus on incarceration in the U.S. does little to repair that.

The restorative justice movement, however, aims to change the direction of criminal law by refocusing it on aiding victims and repairing communities rather than simply incarcerating offenders. Current criminal law focuses on determining which law was broken, who broke it, and what punishment should be meted out. Restorative justice, however, asks: Who was harmed?; How were they harmed?; and How can the offender, community, and criminal justice system help repair the harm? This focus helps the major stakeholders in the event—the victim, offender, and community—focus on moving forward, using the event as a catalyst from which to reengage and empower victims and community members toward building stronger connections. Restorative justice is not any particular program, but a framework for viewing crime and its aftermath.

The following are examples of restorative justice at work:

---

1. "Restoring Dignity, Effecting Justice," by David Lerman from *Human Rights* vol. 26, no. 4, Fall 1999. Reprinted by permission. Copyright © 1999 American Bar Association.

In Minneapolis, the Central City Neighborhood Partnership has begun using a panel of neighborhood residents to meet with offenders charged with soliciting prostitutes. During these sessions, the "john" learns of the effects of prostitution on the neighborhood. Together, the offender and the panel develop a sentence that considers the offender's background and skills, as well as the crime committed. The punishment is usually comprised of (1) community service; (2) a fine; and (3) an education component, and often permits the criminal case to be dismissed if the offender successfully complies with the plan.

In one case, the offender agreed to work with local residents to prepare a community garden for winter, use his sewing skills to mend clothing for a local group home, write an apology letter, and contribute to an organization that helps women escape prostitution. In another case, a young Somalian man arrested for soliciting a prostitute agreed to translate and distribute an educational flier about the ills of prostitution to the Somali community.

A core principle of restorative justice requires that we care about the needs of crime victims. The traditional criminal justice system has slowly become more attuned to the needs of crime victims. For example, many prosecutors' offices now include a victim/witness unit to keep victims informed, and to assist with victims' needs. Some are also moving toward a restorative justice practice called Victim Offender Conferencing (VOC), which allows a victim and offender to meet in a safe setting to actively explore the impact and effect of the crime on their lives. Although the VOC has the flavor of mediation (it is run by a trained facilitator) there is a difference in that the playing field between the parties is not level. Rather, there is an understanding that one party has been wronged, and that the other is there to accept responsibility. The VOC allows the victims to ask questions if they choose to do so. Thus, victims can confront offenders with: "Why me?" and "How did you get in?" Offenders in turn, learn the real human consequences of their actions firsthand. In addition, the VOC enables community members to convey the moral outrage of the community.

During a VOC, it is common for the offender to apologize directly to the victim. Sometimes a victim will forgive the offender for committing the act, although this should never be expected of a victim. Generally, an agreement is reached as to how the offender can repair the harm done. This usually includes a plan for the offender to gain further competencies that will lessen the likelihood of recidivism.

VOC can occur at any point in the criminal justice process. Thus, a conference can be held after a plea, but before sentencing; before a plea, with contemplation of a dismissal or reduced charges on successful completion of the agreed-upon plan; or several years after a criminal act, while the offender is imprisoned.

The following case is a good example of VOC in action:

K.T., an eighteen-year-old high school graduate awaiting entry into a local college where she received an academic scholarship, was working as a cashier at a large grocery store for the summer. Her older brother is in prison, her mother has a cocaine habit, her younger siblings are frequently neglected by their mother who sometimes disappears for days. One day, fed up with her mother's disappearances, K.T. decided to steal money from the store's cash register. The third time she stole money from the store, she was observed pocketing $250. K.T. was arrested and confessed to prior incidents of theft totaling $1,000. She was charged with misdemeanor theft, although the amount stolen could have brought a felony charge. In Milwaukee, a conviction for this offense would have probably landed her probation, with an order to pay restitution, and perhaps jail time of ten to twenty days. Instead, K.T.'s case became one of the test cases for Community Conferencing in Milwaukee, after representatives of the grocery chain agreed to participate. Before a conviction was obtained, the community conference was held, which included K.T., two representatives from the store, K.T.'s attorney, two community members involved with the local Task Force on Restorative justice, and two facilitators.

The facilitated dialogue lasted about one hour, and involved three stages: first, K.T. and the store representatives retold the facts of what happened. Then each party told of the impact the crime had on them. Finally, the parties discussed how to repair the harm caused by the act.

After the facilitator set forth certain guidelines, K.T. spoke first, expressing her remorse and embarrassment through tears. Eventually, the store representatives suggested that K.T. help them by speaking at new employee orientation sessions about the process of getting caught. She also had to make restitution. Because she had no prior record, the prosecutor agreed to dismiss the case if she successfully complied with the agreement reached at the conference.

In another example, in March 1994, the members of Temple B'nai Jeshurun of Des Moines, Iowa, awoke to find neo-Nazi graffiti and swastikas scrawled on their synagogue. Zealous investigation led to the arrest of the perpetrators—a nineteen-year-old male disciple of the Aryan Nation and his seventeen-year-old girlfriend. Neither had a prior record. They were charged with felonies for their hate crime. However, prior to trial, the Temple leadership agreed to meet with the two offenders to explain to them the damage done by their act of hate and to participate in determining how they should be held responsible for their acts.

The offenders pled guilty, and sentencing was put off to accommodate the proposed meeting. A four-hour facilitated session—part of Des Moines' Victim Offender Reconciliation Program (akin to VOC)—was held, during which Temple members, including two Holocaust survivors and a former Israeli military officer, met with the offenders. It soon became clear that the two offenders were classic "wannabes." The boy came from a broken home, was the proverbial "ninety-eight-pound weakling," and had a hearing disability. When he was sixteen, he ran away from home and was taken in by the Aryan Nation. He later returned to Des Moines where he hoped

> *By showcasing the human feelings of compassion, caring, and understanding . . . these VOCs allowed the offenders to truly "learn a lesson," as opposed to merely being warehoused in a prison.*

to become the leader of disparate groups of neo-Nazis in the area. The desecration of the Temple was his first public action against "the enemy." The young woman was extremely unsure of herself. They had been inculcated into neo-Nazi thought as just something to do, without really understanding what it meant.

After much facilitated discussion, the synagogue members and the offenders agreed on the following sentence: 100 hours of service to the synagogue under the supervision of the Temple's custodian, 100 hours of study of Judaism and Jewish history with the Rabbi, a referral to a hearing specialist for the young man, a requirement that the young man remove the Nazi tattoos on his arms, and psychological assessments of both offenders, as well as fulfillment of the requirements for a GED. Because the two offenders did in fact complete their planned activities, the charges were subsequently dismissed.

Using the criminal act as a catalyst on which to build, the VOCs in both cases helped build relationships between alienated individuals and the wider community. By showcasing the human feelings of compassion, caring, and understanding, as opposed to vindictiveness, these VOCs allowed the offenders to truly "learn a lesson," as opposed to merely being warehoused in a prison.

Storytelling is a powerful theme that runs throughout restorative justice principles and practices. The process allows victims and offenders to tell the stories of what really happened and the impact of criminal wrongdoing. By focusing on harm, harm reduction, and accountability, as opposed to simply finding guilt and meting out punishment, restorative justice fosters understanding of the human consequences of crime, and thus, builds human relationships.

This is naturally empowering. Victims are empowered because they feel less fear, which transforms the cycle of fear into an opportunity for hope. The community is empowered because it does not lose an individual to isolation and alienation. Offenders too are empowered by the realization that they are not being treated as throw-away people.

Human rights activists inherently work towards bettering the big picture by working for individuals affected by the power structure. While this is critically important, more can be done. Restorative justice offers a framework by which a criminal act can be used for healing, moving forward, and strengthening communities. As communities become stronger, the cycle of fear caused by crime is transformed into a cycle of hope. The basic human right of being recognized as a vital part of a community regardless of station becomes closer to a reality.

Restorative Justice Resources

Web sites

Center for Restorative Justice and Mediation
http://ssw.che.umn.edu/ctr4rim/

Victim-Offender Mediation Association
http://www.voma.org

Books

Restoring Justice by Daniel Van Ness and Karen Heetderks Strong
Changing Lenses by Howard Zehr

Courts Turning to Public Shaming of Wrongdoers[2]

By Lisa Singhania
Los Angeles Times, April 18, 1999

"Health care fraud does not pay," the full-page newspaper ad warned.

And there in big letters for all to see, federal prosecutors believed, was proof.

In addition to prison time and a fine for billing the government for medical services he did not perform, podiatrist Richard Gorosh of Lansing, Mich., was ordered to announce his guilty plea to the public through full-page ads in two newspapers and a professional journal.

It's a kind of sentencing that's beginning to catch on with prosecutors in federal courts after years of use in lower courts. And it is stoking debate among jurists over what role, if any, public shaming should play in the judicial system as opposed to more traditional sentencing, like prison time.

"The idea of shaming is that it doesn't do society much good to put a productive, nonviolent member of society into jail," said Peter Henning, a professor of criminal law at Wayne State University Law School in Detroit. "But maybe we can benefit from him stating publicly, 'I did this, and this is wrong.' It's sort of like a scarlet letter."

But Andrea Lyon, a professor at the University of Michigan Law School, questions what the ads truly accomplish. She believes tough sentences are the best way to deter crime.

In lower courts, defendants have been ordered to place ads, post signs, wear placards and display bumper stickers telling of such wrongdoing as drunken driving or shoplifting.

But the concept is new in federal courts, where prosecutors are just beginning to use it as a tool in plea agreements with nonviolent criminals.

The U.S. Attorney's Office in western Michigan has used ads in fewer than a half-dozen plea agreements in the last year or so. A Justice Department spokeswoman says she is unaware of any other such ads on the federal level.

---

2. Reprinted with permission of The Associated Press.

Still, Assistant U.S. Attorney Joan Meyer, who works in western Michigan, predicts the ads are here to stay.

"It's not meant to be a public humiliation or putting someone in the stocks," she said. "It has a significant deterrent effect. It sends a message to those who are committing fraud out there . . . that it won't be tolerated."

Among similar punishments in lower courts:

A Utah court in 1996 ordered a convicted drug dealer to post a sign at his home notifying passersby and neighbors of his offense.

A Houston judge in 1997 required a drunken driver to carry a sign outside a bar for five days announcing he killed two people while driving drunk.

An Arkansas judge has sentenced shoplifters to don placards proclaiming their crimes and walk in front of the stores from which they stole.

A Houston judge in 1997 required a drunken driver to carry a sign outside a bar for five days announcing he killed two people while driving drunk.

"I think it's incumbent upon the judiciary to try and be creative—everything else has changed in our society," said Michael Martone, the district judge in Troy who estimates he sentenced 25 to 30 drivers to display the anti-drunken driving bumper stickers in the first two weeks of December.

As part of his plea agreement, Gorosh was sentenced in Kalamazoo by U.S. District Judge Richard Enslen to 14 months in prison and an $80,000 fine—16 times the $5,000 recommended by the government. He also was ordered to pay $110,000 in restitution and to buy the ads, which cost $14,000.

The ads included contact information for readers to report suspected fraud, and about a dozen tips were received from people who read the newspaper ads in the *Grand Rapids Press, Lansing State Journal* and *Journal of the American Podiatric Medical Assn.*, according to federal agencies and insurers.

In court, Judge Enslen questioned whether the ads should be considered a sign of remorse. But afterward, he said they were a good idea.

"I can't prove it, but my gut tells me there's a lot to it. Especially for a white-collar businessperson or physician," Enslen said. "They read newspapers; they listen to the radio."

Still, there is no clear consensus. In a different health care fraud case, prosecutors removed the requirement for ads from a plea bargain recently after U.S. District Judge Robert Holmes Bell questioned their appropriateness.

Bill Mahon, executive director of the National Health Care Anti-Fraud Assn., a Washington nonprofit group, said he doesn't want ads and similar punishment to replace prison sentences or to become common practice. "But added on, who's to say it wouldn't have some benefit?"

Others question the ads' effectiveness.

"I think there's a value in true remorse," said Lyon, of the University of Michigan. "I'm not sure the ad engenders it, although it certainly engenders embarrassment."

The money spent on ads might better be used paying restitution, argued Don Martin, defense lawyer in the health fraud case in which ads were dropped.

But as another defense lawyer, Larry Willey of Grand Rapids, points out, sometimes a defendant does not really have a choice if he is hoping for leniency in court.

"It's never a situation where you want to run the ad," said Willey, who defended two clients who agreed to place ads as part of their federal plea agreements.

As for defendant Gorosh, his words at his sentencing speak for themselves.

"I knew it was wrong and I'm sorry I did it," he said, his head bowed, his voice cracking. "I'm giving up my license. . . . I'm not going to be a podiatrist anymore, and that was important to me.

"If I could take it back, I would."

Old Habits, New Hopes[3]

BY PATRICK ROGERS, RON ARIAS, AND MAUREEN HARRINGTON
PEOPLE WEEKLY, APRIL 23, 2001

Seated in a Los Angeles courtroom, Jakata Arrant fidgets nervously as a judge reads through her case file. Admittedly there is a lot to read. A former runaway, Arrant, 24, has been arrested three times for drugs, most recently in late 1999 for felony possession of cocaine. She acknowledges she has spent roughly half her life desperately addicted—so much so, she says, that on the day of her last release from a state prison, "I was at my dealer's within an hour."

Today, however, Arrant seems to be regaining control of her life, thanks at least in part to the confidence placed in her by superior court Judge Stephen Marcus. In the fall of 1999 Marcus rendered a decision that only a few years ago would have seemed revolutionary. Instead of sending Arrant back to jail, Marcus put her on probation and ordered that she seek treatment at Impact, a West Pasadena rehab center that has counted among its clients Robert Downey Jr. and James Caan. Despite Impact's celebrity cachet, notes Jim Stillwell, who runs the center, it could never be mistaken for a country club. For 12 months Arrant had to adhere to a rigorous schedule of physical labor and group therapy—and make follow-up appearances before Judge Marcus. "She came to us basically from the streets," says Stillwell, himself a recovering addict. "Now she's an employed, responsible mom raising her kids in a healthy, safe, drug-free environment. This is the kind of miracle that motivates me."

Since Arrant was first jailed for using drugs two years ago, much of the nation has begun viewing such crimes differently. Even the most minor drug offenses could once lead to hard time. But with jails and prisons crowded with repeat offenders who can't shake their habits—and given the enormous cost of building new facilities—more and more experts are insisting that drug abuse can't be beaten behind bars. Treatment, they say, is the better option. "We've realized we have been investing our money badly," says Joseph A. Califano, president of the National Center on Addiction and Substance Abuse at Columbia University. "There will always be a need for law enforcement, but the real return will come when we spend on treatment and prevention."

---

3. Patrick Rogers/*People Weekly* © 2001 all rights reserved, Time Inc.

Nowhere has that sentiment had a greater impact than California. With drug offenders making up 30 percent of the state's prison population, voters overwhelmingly approved a bold ballot initiative last fall that abolishes incarceration as a punishment for nearly all nonviolent drug users and instead sends them to state approved treatment centers like Impact. Proposition 36, which becomes law on July 1, clears drug charges from the criminal records of those who graduate from treatment programs and calls for the possibility of jail time only after a third arrest. Supporters of the new law predict that some 36,000 drug users a year will end up in rehab, potentially saving California taxpayers an estimated $200-$250 million in annual prison costs alone, to say nothing of medical, welfare and other costs associated with drug use. But opponents of the proposition, many of whom are in law enforcement, remain unconvinced, pointing to recent studies indicating that as many as half of all addicts who seek treatment relapse.

Arizona, which passed an initiative almost identical to Proposition 36 in 1996, has had mixed results. Adopting a carrot and-stick approach, judges and probation officers have rewarded those who report for court-ordered treatment with small incentives like free museum tickets, while punishing truants with weekend litter-patrol duty. Though angry prosecutors complain that as many as a quarter of all offenders in Maricopa County, the state's most populous, have simply walked away from rehab without fear of ending up behind bars, thousands of others are receiving help for drug problems for the first time. Says Angel Rogers, 46, clinical director of Desert Winds Counseling in Mesa, Ariz., who sees about 40 such clients a week: "I'm pretty positive about the new law. I was expecting a much more resistant clientele, but our statistics show that 76 percent of them are successfully completing treatment. That's a very high number."

Perhaps no recent case better illustrates the uphill struggle faced by chronic users than that of actor Robert Downey Jr., who was arrested on drug-possession charges at a Palm Springs hotel on Nov. 25, not quite four months after his release from a California state prison where he had spent nearly a year. Police say that Downey, now 36, who has pleaded not guilty, was found with nearly 4 grams of cocaine and 16 tranquilizers in his hotel room. If convicted, he could be sent back to prison for up to 56 months, although prosecutors have indicated a willingness to at least consider sending him back to rehab. While cautiously optimistic that Downey could eventually kick his habit, Stillwell, who briefly treated him in the late '90s, says that motivation will be the deciding factor: "Downey has to want it bad."

Though Stillwell, 54, has some reservations about California's new law, believing that the threat of jail time can sometimes prove an effective motivator, he is an absolute convert to the powers of treatment. "As a recovering addict myself," he says, "I'm completely behind anyone trying to get a foothold in a drug-free way of life through treatment, which can bring great hope and strength."

In fact, since enrolling at Impact as a struggling heroin user 27 years ago, he has turned the treatment center into one of the most respected facilities in the country, with a remarkable record in treating addiction.

Of the 400 clients referred by drug courts each year, about 70 percent complete the program and remain arrest-free for life, says [Jim] Stillwell.

Of the 400 clients referred by drug courts each year, about 70 percent complete the program and remain arrest-free for life, says Stillwell. "We've had every type of person in here—judges, airline pilots, thieves, arsonists—and we treat them all the same," he says. Stillwell has developed a one-size-fits-all philosophy that teaches addicts to check their egos at the door and learn to depend on each other in order to kick a habit that, if unchecked, will likely lead to jail or an early grave. He has also chosen to staff his eight facilities with former addicts, because they know the ins and outs of fighting addiction. Says Michael Judge, L.A. County's chief public defender: "We've had phenomenal success with drug addicts, and in great measure this is due to the work of treatment providers like Impact."

Stillwell's effectiveness is largely the product of having conquered his own demons. He was born in Hollywood and raised in Sherman Oaks, Calif., by his mother, Elvira, now 80, and his late father, Jack, a World War II flier who won decorations for heroism in Burma but lapsed into alcoholism on his return home. Stillwell's parents divorced when he was in his teens, and Jim and his sister Nancy, now 47, rarely saw their father after that. "He was tough and gruff," says Jim, "yet he had this sweetness to him. Maybe some of that carried over to me."

Stillwell traces his own history of drug use back to sniffing gasoline in the seventh grade. "I grew up at a time when we thought, 'Once an addict, always an addict,'" he says. As if to prove the point, Stillwell, who dropped out of Catholic high school in 10th grade, tried every drug available-marijuana, cocaine, heroin—often stealing and scamming to fuel his habit. After several arrests and stays in county jail, he volunteered in 1967 for Army service in Vietnam in an attempt to clean up his life.

He might just as well have gone back to the street. On Stillwell's first day with his new infantry company outside Saigon, a dazed-looking GI sauntered up to him and said, "Hey, dude, want some acid?" Stillwell knew his plan to get straight was doomed. "I got loaded and stayed loaded pretty much for my year's tour of duty," he says. Back home in California he encountered the same awkward silences and veiled hostility that bedeviled many Vietnam vets he knew—compounded in Stillwell's case by guilt over his father's death from cancer in 1985. Heroin was his solace until, after hitting rock bottom in 1973 and realizing he couldn't kick his habit, he signed up for treatment at Impact, then a fledgling rehab facility founded three years earlier by a pair of recovering addicts.

Stillwell's first stay at Impact, then located in West L.A., was a disaster. He resented the strict regulations detailing how clients should hang up their clothes and balked when demerits were given out for dust found under the beds. Twice, Stillwell dropped out of the program and got back into drugs. Finally, on his third try, he was sent with a group of other recovering addicts on a weekend camping trip to Big Bear, three hours east of L.A. With no place to score heroin, Stillwell had to go cold turkey. "I've never been so sick in my life," he says. "I was just a curled-up ball on the floor, head in the sink, rocking back and forth. Every joint ached and howled."

Nobody in the group took pity, but neither did they turn their backs on him. "All the guys were there for me, all 20 of them," he says. "They held me. They laughed. They said, 'Come on, punk, get up.' And I was just dying. But they never gave up on me." Back at Impact, Stillwell found added strength in the 12 steps of Narcotics Anonymous. And it didn't hurt that he fell in love. Debi Van Dyck, now 53 and Impact's human resources coordinator, was then a single mother who had started off with diet pills in her 20s, quickly losing control of her life. One night in the early '70s she rear-ended a car and was arrested with 1,000 barbiturates in her possession. After she had logged a half-dozen stays at the L.A. County women's prison while her parents took care of her two children, she enrolled herself in Impact and stayed for 17 months. "Jim had gotten there a week or so before me," she recalls. "At Impact everyone has a job, and if you're new, they start you with washing the pots and pans. That's where we met."

Jim and Debi married two years later, after reclaiming Debi's two daughters: Angela, now 34, who works as an assistant to her mother, and Marci, 30, a homemaker. Together the couple had a third child, Jessica, 22, now a senior at Azusa Pacific University in Azusa, Calif., and raised them all as one family. They consider the kids their greatest source of strength. "We have all the issues that every family has," admits Debi, who goes to a Narcotics Anonymous meeting once a week. "My middle child, Marci, became bulimic. I had no idea what that was, but we worked it out. My oldest daughter has two kids, and when she got a divorce she came here to live. I was happy to help." Jim's mother, who has fibromyalgia, a chronic pain syndrome, moved into the guesthouse of Stillwell's six-bedroom Spanish-style home in Alta Loma in 1993. "You know," says Debi with a smile, "Jim and I used to be the losers. Now we take care of everyone."

Driven by his mission, Jim Stillwell says he has never seriously considered working anywhere but Impact, where he was named director in 1980. Perhaps it's because he needs Impact as much as it needs him. "We addicts have one common denominator," he says. "If we continue to use drugs, we all die. When you understand that, you finally get what we do here."

A New Model to Deal with Crime and Its Victims: Forgiveness[4]

By Jane Lampman
Christian Science Monitor, February 4, 1999

Betty Menkin and her family are learning to forgive the "unforgivable." In doing so, they not only have renewed their own lives but also transformed that of the woman who wronged them.

They found the door to forgiveness and healing through a victim-offender mediation program, an approach to criminal justice that focuses on restitution and restoration.

Betty's sister, Elaine Myers, was killed by a drunk driver while heading home from a night-school class. The circle of grief—and rage—encompassed Ms. Myers's husband, her parents, three sisters and their families. It did not help that the driver, a single mother of two, had a prior drunken-driving conviction.

When Myers's father, Peter Serrell, decided to try the mediation program, none of the others wanted to join in. But as the work progressed under the guidance of Marty Price of the Victim Offender Reconciliation Program (VORP) in Clackamas County, Ore., the entire family gradually got involved.

When their session with the remorseful offender took place months later, they agreed on a program designed—while she was in prison—to free her from alcohol, make her a better parent, get her high school equivalency degree, and involve her in educating others on the dangers of drinking. She wrote them regularly on her progress, and they petitioned for an early parole. The process freed the family from the grip of the past.

Part of a rapidly growing movement called "restorative justice," victim-offender programs show that forgiveness can play a healing role with regard to crime, enabling victims to go on with their lives and helping offenders face their actions and grapple with their futures.

---

4. This article first appeared in *The Christian Science Monitor* on February 4, 1999, and is reproduced with permission. Copyright © 1999 *The Christian Science Monitor*. All rights reserved. Online at *csmonitor.com*.

Emotional Well-Being

The instances that occur in some of these programs corroborate the growing body of academic research on the power of forgiveness. Studies show that it has a marked effect on emotional well-being and aspects of physical health, as well as opening the door to sometimes remarkable instances of reconciliation. Attention is being given not only to its potential for strengthening family life, but also for community and international relations.

Forgiveness is not a goal of mediation programs, nor should it be, those involved emphasize. It arises within the space provided by the process, rather than being part of the agenda.

"Forgiveness has a place, but it should never be imposed, nor should someone feel under a burden to do so," says Howard Zehr, professor of sociology and restorative justice at Eastern Mennonite University in Harrisonburg, Va. "Forgiveness is a gift, and when it happens, it frees people. . . . They talk about being in control of the experience for the first time."

Kate Hunter, who was director of a VORP in Seattle for eight years, says, "I see forgiveness on a continuum—it's something one grows into, if and when you are ready." Everyone interviewed cautioned that they have seen well-intentioned people, whether family members or clergy, push victims too quickly to forgive.

While there have always been individuals, often with strong religious convictions, who were moved to forgive those who committed crimes against them, the system doesn't make it easy.

"When you look broadly at the criminal-justice system, there haven't been many opportunities for forgiveness because there haven't been many opportunities for encounter," says Ron Rosenberger of Prison Fellowship Ministries. "Our present system separates people from one another."

Crime is defined as an offense against the state, justice is defined as establishing blame and meting out punishment, and the process is an adversarial one, Dr. Zehr says. It tends to reenforce the hostility resulting from the crime. (Zehr wrote "Changing Lenses," [Herald, 1990] one of the most influential books on restorative justice.)

"The fundamental problem is that it leaves the victim out and it doesn't hold the offender accountable in the sense of understanding the harm they've caused and taking responsibility for it," he says. "When you harm someone, you create an obligation, and that obligation is to make things right."

The victim-offender programs of restorative justice put the crime victim at the center and provide an engagement that humanizes both victim and offender. Each shares their story and explores the impact of the crime in the process of working out a restitution program.

Some 300 programs now exist in the United States, and they are growing by leaps around the world (the first was in Canada). The entire juvenile-justice system of New Zealand is based on restorative justice. Victim-offender programs have primarily focused on juvenile cases, but in recent years have moved into adult and even serious violent crime.

Bruce Kittle, director of the restorative-justice project at the University of Wisconsin Law School at Madison, handled a case of attempted homicide whose impact has reached beyond the individuals involved.

Two teenagers planning to run away were trying to steal a car from a rural home when the woman caught them. They shot her, leaving her blind and partially paralyzed. The woman went through the program with the youngster who pulled the trigger. A woman of faith, she said she experienced two levels of forgiveness. She decided not to hate them soon after the crime, although she was still angry. But when she sat down with a deeply remorseful, apologetic, and sobbing young man two years later, it "lifted her to a second level of forgiveness."

Now, she goes to a maximum-security prison twice a month, where she joins inmates in presenting a "Scared Straight" program to juvenile offenders. "A lot of the men have done terrible things and are in for long sentences," Mr. Kittle says. "Not only has she impacted the young people that visit the program, she has profoundly impacted the inmates . . . talking with them about reclaiming their own sense of humanity."

Inmates Struggle with Forgiveness

Forgiveness is an issue for inmates as well as for victims. "Most of the guys I meet with, forgiveness is pretty important to them," Kittle says. "Some are really struggling from a faith perspective about forgiveness vis-à-vis themselves and a Creator, but also they understand that that is related . . . to forgiveness between them and the victim."

Zehr tells of an intensive program he was involved with in a Pennsylvania maximum-security prison working with lifers to help them take responsibility for what they had done. "The question of forgiveness just came up in dramatic fashion. . . . When they'd meet with victims who weren't their own, they'd ask, 'Do I have the right to ask forgiveness?'"

An offender's apology is a regular aspect of mediation sessions. (Only those who admit guilt can participate in the programs.) If they go a step further and ask for forgiveness, "the power shift is really dynamic," Kittle says. "You can feel it in the room. The offender says to the victim, 'You don't have to respond to this, I just want you to know that your someday forgiving me is really important. . . . Whatever the victim says, the victim has control."

Ray Anderson, professor of theology and ministry at Fuller Theological Seminary in Pasadena, Calif., wrote a book some years ago called "The Gospel According to Judas: Is There a Limit to God's Forgiveness?" He heard from several in prison who had read it,

---

> ### *Research under way on forgiveness includes its potential in coping with violence and crime.*

---

including a convicted murderer in Los Angeles who asked him to visit.

"Manacled to the bench, he pulled out his copy and read to me parts that meant something to him. He had felt terrible remorse for years. Then he asked, 'Can God ever forgive me for murdering my own parents?'"

Dr. Anderson asked him if he thought his mother would forgive him. After a long pause, he said he thought she would. "I said, 'Then you know that God would.' He responded, 'Now I can try to make something of my life even though in prison.'"

Research under way on forgiveness includes its potential in coping with violence and crime. It has already proved effective in reducing levels of anger.

Studies indicate that a large proportion of those in prison were physically or sexually abused as children. They think of themselves as victims of that and of the system. "When some guys learn the pain they have caused someone, their own pain is so deep that it's hard for them to develop empathy for others," Kittle says. Getting at that first could help, he adds.

Robert Enright, who created the Institute for Forgiveness Research at the University of Wisconsin, is conducting a study with sexual predators. Traditional therapy has proven ineffective with them—they show no empathy whatsoever. His program tries to help them to forgive people in their own past who have hurt them. If they can develop empathy in that process, they may be able to look at their victims and others with empathy.

In our society today, "we've just disconnected ourselves from the criminal-justice system," Kittle says. We put people in jail and think "that takes care of it. Yet 95 percent . . . eventually get out."

That means programs that help people on both sides of a crime can also make a difference for the community. The Serrell family's work with the young alcoholic became what Price calls "a healing alliance." Now he says, "I'm coming to see the healing alliance as something that in many cases can be expected to happen. And it may have benefits far beyond what mediation itself can accomplish."

Kittle is working on another kind of "healing alliance." He is trying to involve churches in mentoring prisoners when they are released. "For me, it connects to forgiveness and the possibility of redemption for people—it helps create community for them. Research shows that the more people feel connected to a community, the less likely they are to commit a crime."

Bibliography

Books

Blomberg, Thomas G., and Karol Lucken. *American Penology: A History of Control*. Hawthorne, NY: Aldine de Gruyter, 2000.

Burton-Rose, Daniel, Dan Pens, and Paul Wright. *The Celling of America: An Inside Look at the U.S. Prison Industry*. Monroe, ME: Common Courage Press, 1998.

Carlson, Norman A., Karen M. Hess, and Christine M. H. Orthmann. *Corrections in the 21st Century: A Practical Approach*. Belmont, CA: West/Wadsworth, 1999.

Christianson, Scott. *With Liberty for Some: 500 Years of Imprisonment in America*. Boston: Northeastern University Press, 1998.

Craig, Russell L., and David A. Rausch. *A Historical, Philosophical, and Pragmatic Approach to Penology*. Lewiston: E. Mellen Press, 1994.

Currie, Elliott. *Crime and Punishment in America*. New York: Metropolitan Books, 1998.

Feeley, Malcolm M., and Edward L. Rubin. *Judicial Policy Making and the Modern State: How the Courts Reformed America's Prisons*. New York: Cambridge University Press, 1998.

Freeman, Robert M. *Popular Culture and Corrections*. Lanham, MD: American Correctional Association, 2000.

Grapes, Bryan J., ed. *Prisons*. San Diego: Greenhaven Press, 2000.

Haas, Kenneth C., and Geoffrey P. Alpert, eds. *The Dilemmas of Corrections: Contemporary Readings*. Prospect Heights, IL: Waveland Press, 1999.

Hallinan, Joseph T. *Going up the River: Travels in a Prison Nation*. New York: Random House, 2001.

Hirsch, Adam Jay. *The Rise of the Penitentiary: Prisons and Punishment in Early America*. New Haven: Yale University Press, 1992.

Hugunin, James R. *A Survey of the Representation of Prisoners in the United States: Discipline and Photographs—the Prison Experience*. Lewiston: Edwin Mellen Press, c1999.

Johnson, Robert. *Hard Time: Understanding and Reforming the Prison*. Belmont, CA: Wadsworth, 2001.

Keve, Paul W. *Prisons and the American Conscience: A History of U.S. Federal Corrections*. Carbondale: Southern Illinois University Press, 1991.

McShane, Marilyn, and Frank P. Williams III, eds. *The Philosophy and Practice of Corrections*. New York: Garland Pub., 1997.

Morris, Norval,and David J. Rothman, eds. *The Oxford History of the Prison: The Practice of Punishment in Western Society*. New York: Oxford University Press, 1995.

Parenti, Christian. *Lockdown America: Police and Prisons in the Age of Crisis*. New York: Verso, 2001.

Pisciotta, Alexander W. *Benevolent Repression: Social Control and the American Reformatory-Prison Movement*. New York: New York University Press, 1994.

Roberts, John W. *Reform and Retribution: An Illustrated History of American Prisons*. Lanham, MD: American Correctional Association, 1997.

Schmidt, Peter, and Ann D. Witte. *An Economic Analysis of Crime and Justice: Theory, Methods, and Applications*. Orlando: Academic Press, 1984.

Shelden, Randall G. *Controlling the Dangerous Classes: A Critical Introduction to the History of Criminal Justice*. Boston: Allyn and Bacon, 2001.

Shichor, David, and Michael J. Gilbert, eds. *Privatization in Criminal Justice: Past, Present, and Future*. Cincinnati: Anderson Pub., 2001.

Skotnicki, Andrew. *Religion and the Development of the American Penal System*. Lanham, MD: University Press of America, 2000.

Welch, Michael. *Punishment in America: Social Control and the Ironies of Imprisonment*. Thousand Oaks, CA: Sage Publications, 1999.

Additional Periodical Articles with Abstracts

More information on the American prison system can be found in the following articles. Readers who require a more comprehensive selection are advised to consult *Reader's Guide Abstracts* and other H.W. Wilson indexes.

Dealing with Drugs. William J. Fitzpatrick. *Albany Times Union* pB1 May 16, 1999.

Fitzpatrick writes, "As we enter the 21st century, a small but media-savvy group of 'enlightened' policy thinkers is calling for repeal of the Rockefeller Drug Laws so, the argument goes, our prisons will not be bursting at the seams with nonviolent drug offenders. . . . They are well-intentioned but mis-focused. The fact that only 1.4 percent of current state prison inmates fall into the category of first-time, nonviolent drug offenders has so far failed to deter these apologists." He also asserts, "Drugs are evil and those who profit from pushing drugs are violent people engaged in a violence-prone business."

Public-Private Partnerships in the U.S. Prison System. Anne Larason Schneider. *American Behavioral Scientist* v.43 pp192–208 Sep. 1999

Schneider explains that public-private partnerships in the operation of prisons have existed from the colonial period to contemporary times, although the extent of reliance on the private sector and the policy design models have varied somewhat. Drawing on ideas from policy design theory, this study identifies the characteristics of the partnerships, the reasons for private-sector involvement, the rationales and claims made by competing perspectives, and the consequences of private-sector involvement. Prison policy differs from other policy arenas in ways that have implications for the appropriate role of the private sector because, within a prison, every aspect of an inmate's life is disciplined and subject to enhanced punishment at the discretion of guards and other personnel.

Justice Gets a Fresh Look. Marcella Bombardieri. *Boston Globe* ppB1–2 Nov. 27, 1999.

Bombardieri reports that, for the past year, Franklin County, Massachusetts, has been experimenting with a "restorative justice" program that brings offenders, their victims, and members of the community face to face to discuss the harm a particular crime inflicted and how that harm can be repaired. One goal of the national restorative justice movement is to give victims a voice in the justice system. Another is to transform the lives of offenders, bestowing new hope and resources upon substance abusers and wayward teenagers. While such talk may sound like nothing more than a do-gooder's daydream, the program in Greenfield and Orange district courts has been successful enough that at least two offenders who came before "restorative probation boards" have been asked to join the boards as community members who hear cases.

A New Economic Reality: Penal Keynesianism. L. Randall Wray. *Challenge* v.43 pp31–59 Sep./Oct. 2000.

Wray examines the pros and cons of using prison labor. Many institutions deduct a portion of their employed prisoners' pay in order to fund room and board, thus relieving some of the costs of maintaining prisons. Some studies show that prisoners who work have a better chance of getting a job upon their release, and therefore of keeping out of trouble. Wray concludes, however, that prison labor steals jobs from undereducated young males, the same group that is already at the highest risk of being incarcerated.

Town Needs Revitalizing? Build a Prison. Debre Guillaume. *Christian Science Monitor* p3 Apr. 5, 2000.

Guillaume reports that the largest prison building boom in U.S. history is proving to be a boon to many small towns across the country. From New York to California, billions of dollars have been put into bricks, bars, and concertina wire in the past 20 years as the number of federal, state, and city-run penitentiaries has soared. Many of them have been located in rural areas. While many towns have traditionally fought the presence of prisons in their backyard—and some local residents still do—a growing number now see them as a way to revitalize their communities. High unemployment rates have reduced much of the reticence in rural America. Indeed, prisons are now often synonymous with job opportunities, new infrastructures, and investment.

Can Tolerance Be Taught? Eric Tischler. *Corrections Today* v.61 pp76–79 Aug. 1999.

Tischler writes that, according to author Jack Levin, the typical hate crime offender is a first-time offender, or "a teenager who goes out to bash." Levin estimates that no more than 5% of hate crimes are committed by organized hate groups, but that these groups are most likely to be involved in the most serious crimes.

Fanning the Flames of Fear. John Irwin, James Austin, et al. *Crime & Delinquency* v.44 pp32–48 Jan. 1998.

The writers argue that beginning with Richard Nixon, politicians have benefitted greatly from campaigns that promise to get tough on crime by locking up as many people as possible, regardless of the social or economic costs to our society. It has been an ideal issue for them. They can always get the majority of Americans riled up about crime, and there is virtually no constituency who opposes reducing crime. Those who have opposed this punitive policy have been quickly labeled as liberals who are soft on crime and are actually contributing to the level of violence that plagues our society.

The Story Nobody Talks About: The Shocking Plight of Black Women Prisoners. Kimberly Davis. *Ebony* v.55 pp162–166 June 2000.

Davis reports that a Black woman in America is seven times more likely to be imprisoned than a White woman, according to the U.S. Department of Justice's Bureau of Labor Statistics. She notes that Black women prisoners must cope with racism, drug addiction, sexual exploitation, pregnancy and motherhood, and a system that often is not set up with women in mind.

The Forgotten Prisoners of a Disastrous War. Mary Frances Berry. *Essence* v.30 p194 Oct. 1999.

Berry reports on the case of Karen Blakney, 29, who faced a ten-year mandatory minimum prison sentence for making crack. She considered herself lucky when the judge gave her only 33 months. She served her time, underwent drug treatment successfully, and even moved on to hold down a legitimate job. Still, a tough-on-crime U.S. attorney initiated a series of appeals to force Blakney's sentence up to the ten-year minimum, even pressuring this working mother, now 38, to return to the streets as an informant in exchange for staying out of prison. Blakney's plight, Berry argues, illustrates how Black women have increasingly joined Black men as fodder for the "prison-industrial complex" that creates jobs for one part of the economy at the expense of freedom and opportunity for another. If society had wanted to use the legal system to make war on poor Black women and their children, it could have chosen no better weapons than the shameful "war on drugs."

Crackdown on Inmate Phone Use Sought As States Rake in Millions. Joseph T. Hallinan. *Houston Chronicle* p38 Aug. 29, 1999.

Hallinan demonstrates that in the running of our prisons, profit motive and security can sometimes be at odds with each other. At Menard Correctional Center in Illinois, one inmate, Gustavo Colon, used prison phones to orchestrate drug sales on the street. Though Colon was later caught, Hallinan points out that states stand to gain much from letting prisoners have full use of phones. The state of Illinois receives 50 percent of inmate phone charges, which amounted to $12.2 million in 1998.

Making Life Miserable for Felons: Co-founder Propels Victims' Rights Group into Heart of Issues. Allan Turner. *Houston Chronicle* pA36 June 11, 2000.

Turner reports on the 4,000-member Justice for All, a victim's rights group. The group successfully has pushed for measures that make life harder for convicted offenders. Denying violent felons' release on bond while they pursue appeals, ending the "mandatory release" policy for new inmates, improving a still-flawed system of tracking sexual predators once they've been freed from prison—all have been signal legislative victories for the Houston-based group. Its unequivocal stand on issues such as capital punishment—the group favors the death penalty and supported the controversial execution of Houston's Gary Graham—propels Justice for All into the heart of the era's most divisive issues.

Texas Prisons after the Reforms. Kathy Walt. *Houston Chronicle* pA3 Mar. 30, 1999.

Walt visits a high-security prison near Huntsville, Texas. Here prisoners are kept in near complete isolation in six-foot by nine-foot cells. Some say this form of treatment is the best option for problematic inmates, while others say it can only make sick men sicker.

Against Mandatory Minimums. John J. DiIulio Jr. *National Review* v.51 pp46–51 May 17, 1999.

DiIulio argues that there is a conservative crime-control case to be made for repealing mandatory-minimum drug laws. Though he initially supported mandatory-minimums, he has come to oppose them and favors drug treatment programs instead. Since the mid 1990s, DiIulio notes, a large group of New York's incoming prison population has consisted of offenders whose only past felony crimes, recorded and undetected, were genuinely low-level, nonviolent drug crimes. Many of these "drug-only offenders," as he term them, are themselves drug abusers or addicts who have never been in a well-structured, no-nonsense, community-anchored substance-abuse program.

In "Super Max," Terms of Endurance. James Brooke. *New York Times* p38 June 13, 1999.

Brooke describes how the Administrative Maximum Facility in Florence, Colorado, has won national attention for its "bomber wing," a unit that keeps under multiple locks and keys Timothy J. McVeigh, the Oklahoma City bomber, Theodore J. Kaczynski, the Unabomber, and Ramzi Ahmed Yousef, the mastermind of the World Trade Center bombing. Of the men sent here, in what officials call a control unit prison, 35 percent have committed murder in prison, 41 percent have tried to escape, and 85 percent have committed assaults in prison. Almost 75 prisoners have graduated from the prison, winning transfer to less-restrictive prisons. In addition, by concentrating highly violent prisoners here, prison violence has dropped across the Federal prison system.

U.S. Figures Show Prison Population Is Now Stabilizing. David Firestone. *New York Times* pA1 June 9, 2001.

Firestone reports that after growing explosively for three decades, the nation's prison population has begun to stabilize, according to new government figures. For the first time in years, the overcrowding that has plagued state prisons and local jails alike is beginning to ease, as a result of falling crime rates and a decade of new construction. Through the middle of last year, the number of state prisoners grew by only 1.5 percent, the lowest annual increase in 29 years, according to figures recently compiled by the United States Department of Justice. Government officials and other experts in the field say there are several reasons for the slowing growth, but the most important is that the prison system is finally experiencing the benefits of the decline in crime rates that began in the mid-1990s.

Prison Conversion. Jacob Sullum. *Reason* v.31 pp40–48 Aug./Sep. 1999.

Sullum describes several instances in which the punishments issued for drug crimes seem out of proportion to the gravity of the crimes. He goes on to evaluate U.S. drug policy as it relates to prisons, noting that, even among former supporters, mandatory minimums for drug violations are being questioned.

Rolling Back Three Strikes. Gary Delsohn and Sam Stanton. *Salon.com* May 9, 2000.

The authors examine mandatory sentencing laws in California that are currently in question. Three strikes laws, which impose maximum sentences for repeat offenders, have caused major logistical problems in California, which holds more inmates than do France, Great Britain, Germany, Japan, Singapore, and the Netherlands combined. Consequently, three strikes laws are about to be scaled back.

Slaves to the System. Nina Siegal. *Salon.com* Sep. 1, 1998.

Siegal offers in-depth looks at the lives of several women prisoners. In these female prisons, overseen mostly by male guards, there is an overwhelming prevalence of rape.

Drug Treatment Takes Time to Succeed. Robert Collier. *San Francisco Chronicle* pA17 June 24, 2001.

Collier points out that Proposition 36, California's new drug treatment plan that is intended to replace prison terms for many addicts, will not be an instant success. "It's ridiculous to expect instant recovery," said Steven Loveseth, a substance abuse program manager and chair of Contra Costa County's task force to oversee implementation of Proposition 36. Loveseth said his own experience is proof that the demons of addiction cannot be shaken easily. A former heroin addict, Loveseth went through five bouts of treatment over a period of several years, relapsing again and again into drug use until he went permanently "clean and sober" in 1983.

Inmates Sue State over Health Care. Bob Egelko. *San Francisco Chronicle* pA3 Apr. 6, 2001.

Egelko reports on a suit billed as the largest class-action ever filed over prison conditions, in which nine inmates and their lawyers claimed the system's health care suffers from poor training, staff shortages, delays in access to doctors and tests, interference by guards and defective care for HIV-positive prisoners. Criticism of prison health care has mounted as the state inmate population has grown. Last fall, in a hearing at Valley State Prison for Women in Chowchilla (Madera County), legislators heard accounts of medical mistreatment and neglect from a dozen female inmates.

Locking up the Vote. Nicholas Thompson. *Washington Monthly* pp17–21 Jan./Feb. 2001.

Thompson examines how, under Florida law, every felon is permanently barred from the voting booth. According to the best available estimates, this law kept 525,000 people in Florida, most of them poor and a great many of them African-American, away from the polls in a presidential election decided by just a few hundred votes. Thompson discusses the disenfranchisement of former prisoners in Florida.

Index